Advance Pra  *)ots*

"A breath of fresh air in a world of endless 'how to' parenting books."
—Jerry Finkelstein, Ph.D., Director, The New School Counseling Center

"A great source of support, encouragement, and practical ideas to inspire parents and caregivers."
—Andrew Malekoff, author of *Group Work with Adolescents* (Guilford, 2014); Executive Director and CEO, North Shore Child and Family Guidance Center; and Editor-in-Chief, Social Work with Groups

"A much needed resource for parents of children all ages."
—Amy Margolis, Ph.D., Columbia University Medical Center, and Director of Neuropsychology, Brooklyn Learning Center

"An enlightened, no-nonsense approach to navigating the blind curves of parenting."
—Gina Barnett, author of *Play the Part: Mastering Body Signals to Connect and Communicate for Business Success* (McGraw-Hill, 2015)

"If you are desperate to get your relationships with your kid back on track— read this book. In fact, read it twice!"
—Bob Townley, Founder and Executive Director, Manhattan Youth

"A creative blend of kid smarts, common sense, and compassion for parents."
—Robert Bolton, author of *People Skills*, *People Styles at Work and Beyond*, and others

"This book is so great, it's like having Sean Grover in my linen closet for daily affirmations!"
—Kate Harrison, VP Exec Bd PTA, Lower Manhattan Community School

"The ultimate book to parents who need guidance. Incisive, forceful, simply written, and useful to any parent."
—George Weinberg, Ph.D., author of *The Heart of Psychotherapy*

"A handy go-to manual for parents when turbulent waters threaten smooth sailing."
—Bill Santiago, comedian and author of *Pardon my Spanglish*

"The perfect companion for any parent."
—Penny Ekstein-Lieberman, President/CEO Toot Sweet Toys Inc.

For my parents, Al and Rosemarie.

"It may seem that parents teach the child, but in the end it is the other way around. Bringing up children is a way for parents to become more complete themselves."

—Daisaku Ikeda

When kids call the shots

how to seize control from your darling
bully—and enjoy being a parent again

Sean Grover

AMACOM AMERICAN MANAGEMENT ASSOCIATION

New York ▸ Atlanta ▸ Brussels ▸ Chicago ▸ Mexico City ▸ San Francisco
Shanghai ▸ Tokyo ▸ Toronto ▸ Washington, D.C.

Bulk discounts available. For details visit: www.amacombooks.org/go/specialsales
Or contact special sales:
Phone: 800-250-5308 / Email: specialsls@amanet.org
View all the AMACOM titles at: www.amacombooks.org
American Management Association: www.amanet.org

This publication is designed to provide accurate and authoritative information in regard to the subject matter covered. It is sold with the understanding that the publisher is not engaged in rendering legal, accounting, or other professional service. If legal advice or other expert assistance is required, the services of a competent professional person should be sought.

None of the people mentioned in the profiles in this book actually exist; the names, genders and ages have been changed to protect privacy and honor confidentiality. Any resemblance to actual persons is strictly coincidental.

Grover, Sean.
When kids call the shots : how to seize control from your darling bully—and enjoy being a parent again / Sean Grover.
    pages cm
Includes index.
ISBN 978-0-8144-3600-4 (pbk.) — ISBN 978-0-8144-3601-1 (ebook) 1. Parenting—Psychological aspects. 2. Parent and child. 3. Bullying. 4. Control (Psychology) I. Title.
HQ755.8.G758 2015
306.874—dc23
                                                              2014049981

About AMA

American Management Association (www.amanet.org) is a world leader in talent development, advancing the skills of individuals to drive business success. Our mission is to support the goals of individuals and organizations through a complete range of products and services, including classroom and virtual seminars, webcasts, webinars, podcasts, conferences, corporate and government solutions, business books, and research. AMA's approach to improving performance combines experiential learning—learning through doing—with opportunities for ongoing professional growth at every step of one's career journey.

Printing number
10 9 8 7 6 5 4 3 2 1

contents

acknowledgments

I want to thank my mentors, the great Louis Ormont and George Weinberg, for giving me confidence when I had none, and Daisaku Ikeda, who continues to inspire me every day. Thanks also to Lynn Sonberg and Meg Schneider for convincing me to write this book, Carol Mann for believing in it, and Ellen Kadin at AMACOM for her infinite patience and support of this first-time writer.

Special thanks to . . .

My writing teacher and friend, Gina Barnett, who taught me everything (and then some); Aunt Dot & Uncle Bob for editing everything I've ever written since seventh grade; Grandma Grover for her relentless optimism and perfect French toast.

My teachers: Bill Young, Paul Geltner, Lena Furgeri, Michael Brook, Stephen Pagano, Louis Greenstein, the mysterious Mrs. Wolf, Philip Turner, Harry Candelario, Joan Ormont, Dianne Rowe, Richard Cheney, Gary Bron, Didi Goldenhar, Neta Katz, Marianne Fuenmayor, Four Eyes Edit: Margarita Kurtz & Adela Brito, and Spalding Grey.

The cheerleaders: Jennifer Lieber, Jonathan Curelop, Ellen Kealy, Jerry Finkelstein, Bill Santiago, Erin Martin, Bob Townley of Manhattan Youth, Penny Ekstein-Lieberman, Father Arcoleo, Patsy Kettler, Kathy Morrell, Brunette Alcy, Beth Harpaz, Steve McNulty, Josephine Grover, Paris Williams, RUDY LUCAS, Teresa Solomita, Dan Gross, Elizabeth Rovere, David Dumais,

Patty Cox, Chris Dolin, Diana Gasperoni of the Relationship Project, Liza Cooper, Liz Morrison, Suhadee Henriquez, Susan Klett, Fran Carpentier, Matt Lynch; and my brothers and sisters: Al, Dante, Joanna, Andrea, and their massive army of children.

My colleagues at Washington Square Institute and the amazing support staff, my fellow social workers at the late-great Brooklyn Psychiatric Center, and all the school principals, parent coordinators, and guidance counselors in the New York City public and private schools who allowed me to work out the principles in this book in parenting workshops.

My fellow Buddhists: Steven Sater, Adin Strauss, Stephen Kennard, LuAnn Adams, Zoe Richards, Tom Knapp, Douglas Berger, Jarrett Smithwrick, Blane Charles, Dru Barnes, Chuck Gomez, Jorge Reliz, Jessica Jiji, Jeff Ourvan, Michael Royce, Bob Weinstein, Mike Young, Tim McNally, Lenny Rosenblum, Michon Peacock, Bill Thompson, and all the members of SGI family.

For all the establishments who offered me a quiet corner to write: the McBurney YMCA on 14th, Joe's Coffee on 13th, Grumpy's Coffee on 20th, the Lange Cottage in Maine, the Block Island Ferry, the Harbor Inn, Washington Square Institute, the 210 Roof Deck, the SGI-USA New York Culture Center, the Big Blue House in Freeport, Third Street Music School, the waiting room at West 11th Pediatrics, The Red House in Quebec, the Long Island Rail Road, the NYC Subway System, and all the dog parks in Manhattan.

For my patients, who make my work such an adventure and inspiration. I am honored and grateful for our time together.

And, most of all, thanks to my wife, Yuko, and my beautiful, talented daughters, Emma and Mina, for their love and patience in teaching me everything I know about parenting.

Introduction

Something's gone wrong in your relationship with your kid. You can't put your finger on it. You're not sure when it happened, you're not sure how it happened, but you know that you want to make your relationship right again—as soon as possible. There's only one problem: You haven't got a clue what to do.

You coach yourself. "Stay optimistic. It's just a phase. It will pass. Be positive." You cross your fingers and hope for the best.

But such thoughts offer little comfort. When your relationship with your kid is out of whack, "hope" doesn't cut it. In fact, nothing in your life feels right. You spend many sleepless nights feeling brokenhearted and lost. I know—I've been there.

Parenting is a messy business, filled with unexpected turns and twists. You need new skills to overcome these problems—and fast. Even the most devoted parents can feel flummoxed by their kids.

"I thought I was doing everything right. Why is this happening?"

Rebooting Your Relationship

Seeking professional advice is always a good idea, but before you spend hundreds or thousands of dollars on therapy, behavior modification programs, or medication or submit your child to personality assessments and neurological testing, let's consider some steps that you can take right now.

Children are complicated, but their needs are not. As we'll learn in Chapter 2, every child has five basic needs. Meet those five needs, and you'll be amazed at how quickly your kid's behavior and mood improve. However, if those essential needs aren't met, turning around your relationship with your kid could be infinitely more difficult.

Rather than muck up parenting with too much analysis or obsessiveness, let's keep it simple and stick to basics. Often, the solutions to problems in your relationship are hiding in plain sight. In fact, remedying your situation with your kid could be easier than you think.

For example, for quite a while I had a leak under my kitchen sink. No matter what I did, the leak reappeared. Plumbers told me that the pipes were installed wrong, the drain was off center, the sink had to be moved. Each estimate was for hundreds of dollars that I didn't want to spend. After all, it was just a tiny drip!

So I went to my local hardware store and spoke to one of the old-timers. Without missing a beat, he said, "Try changing the washers." He sold me three thirty-five-cent washers. And the pipes never leaked again.

So before you freak out and hire an army of mental health professionals to fix your kid, before you research social workers, psychologists, psychiatrists, or psychotherapists (I'll explain exactly what these folks do in Chapter 7), before you blame yourself or your partner or spend sleepless nights feeling guilty, take a moment and consider this: You don't need to start all over; you might just need to change the washers.

Modern-Day Parenting

Parents today don't dabble in parenting. They work hard to understand their kids; they read parenting books and magazines, listen to parenting podcasts, and attend parenting workshops. Progressive parents don't want anything chancy when it comes to parenting advice.

What's the driving force behind this recent boom in parenting? All good parents want to give their children a better childhood than they had. To me, such dedicated parents are living works of art, masterpieces in parenting. They parent with purpose, passion, and pleasure; they have healthy relationships with their kids because they worked on it and they worked on themselves.

The Healing Work of Parenting

What if you are providing your kids with the basic needs? You're attentive, sensitive, and treat them with respect—and yet your relationship is still calamitous? Then we have to go deeper and search for hidden causes. Finding those causes will require some diligence.

Relationships with children are like any other: They are rarely good by accident, and they always require work. It's only a matter of time before the difficulties you have in adult relationships surface in your relationship with your kid. Bad habits come to the forefront when we become parents. For example, we sometime punish our kids for misbehaving in ways that we ourselves model at home. To avoid having our kids repeat our shortcomings, we need to learn new skills.

In this way, being a parent offers us a chance to repair those damaged parts of ourselves—parts we avoid or prefer to keep out of sight. Disharmony within us fuels disharmony with our children. Happy parents produce happy children, and vice versa. Healing our own internal disharmony is the first step to healing disharmony with our kids.

In parenting sessions, my goal is always to help parents learn to monitor their own thoughts and feelings and hit the pause button before reacting to their kid's problem behaviors. Reactivity without mindfulness escalates arguments, increases conflicts, and disempowers your parenting.

Keeping your relationship with your kid in good shape will also require coming to grips with your history. In the chapters that follow, you'll learn that rejuvenating your relationship with your child starts with digging deep into your past and discovering how it shapes your parenting choices:

> ➤ How were you parented?

> ➤ What did your parents do best?

> ➤ What did your parents fail to do?

A mindful exploration of your experiences, focused on the feelings and impulses that you experience today as a parent, will help you develop greater attunement, understanding, and empathy. You will grasp your kid's experience more quickly and respond with more understanding and compassion. Understanding breeds intimacy and respect; children who feel understood by their parents rarely push them away.

➤ ➤ ➤

Many years ago in a bookstore, I attended an interview with one of my favorite authors. Bone-thin and frail, he toddled over to the microphone. The interviewer's first question was, "What do you consider your greatest accomplishment?"

He had won almost every award a writer could win, so I thought of a number of ways he could answer this question. Would he say his Pulitzer Prize–winning play? His Academy award–nominated film scripts?

Without missing a beat, he replied, "My children."

In that moment I learned a valuable lesson: There is no greater accomplishment than raising well-adjusted children and enjoying healthy relationships with them.

That's why I wrote this book. It's for parents who, when faced with challenges, are willing to work on themselves and strive to create a better a relationship with their kids. It's for parents who are determined to give their kids the best childhood that they can.

The rewards of good parenting flow back into our own lives. Nothing is more fulfilling than sending a happy child into the world unburdened by a troubled home life, resentments, or acquired bad habits—free to be themselves, purely and unfettered. Such a healthy relationship is the greatest gift that we give to our children—and ourselves.

chapter one

Escape the suffering parents club

Welcome! If you bought this book, chances are, your kid has bullied you. I'm not talking about occasional backtalk that comes along with every phase of child development. I'm talking about children actually abusing their parents.

How on earth does this happen?

A generation or two ago, it would have been unthinkable for children to bully their parents. Chances are, you would never have attempted to push around your mother or father. In fact, many parents are quick to tell me that they feared challenging their parent's authority.

Yet today, everyone knows a parent who is bullied. Pay a visit to your local playground or stroll through a shopping mall, and you're bound to see the bullied parent dynamic in action—a child yelling, cursing, or even hitting a parent. For bullied parents, the terrible twos never end; they simply morph into the terrible tween, the terrible teen, the terrible college student, and beyond.

For relief, we may turn to blame. We can point a finger at genetics or family history; perhaps we fault society, our partner (or ex-partners), or even ourselves. But such tactics rarely produce value. They provide no guidelines for repairing our relationship and only reinforce our sense of being victimized by our kids.

Bullying at home is a symptom of imbalance within the entire family. Perhaps there has been some disruptive event, such as a divorce, illness, or financial hardship. Maybe your child is going through a difficult developmental phase. There may have been an upsetting transition, such as relocating or starting at a new school. Trials like these can raise overwhelming insecurities in kids and fuel bullying behaviors.

On Being a Parent

Once, parenting was an afterthought, something to be checked off your things-grownups-do list on your way to retirement. To make matters worse, we had lots of lousy proverbs to screw up our view of childrearing:

"Children should be seen and not heard."

"Spare the rod, spoil the child."

"Do as I say, not as I do."

Is it any surprise that these phrases were coined in medieval times? No doubt, we pay a heavy price for such unenlightened views of parenting.

So before we delve into the complex world of the bullied parent, I'd like to applaud you for taking the work of parenting so seriously.

If you're reading this now, you are a member of a new generation of parents who recognize the importance of self-awareness and mindfulness when it comes to raising an emotionally healthy child.

Becoming a parent is a life-altering event, one that initiates a profound transformation on every level of your consciousness. It's impossible to become a parent without your identity going through a startling overhaul.

While the joys of parenting are frequently highlighted, its anxieties are often overlooked. Becoming a parent has an enormous effect on our relationships, personalities, and behaviors. It also introduces new pressures that we never saw coming, such as monetary challenges, time management issues, or health problems. Parents find themselves sleeping less, worrying more, and struggling with feelings that they don't understand.

From the start, parenting stirs up our own childhood experiences, which can shake us to the core. We may find ourselves saying things our parents said, escalating conflicts with our children, or recreating problematic aspects of our relationships with our own parents.

Let's go back to the bullying child in the playground or the mall. From a distance, it looks like an angry child pushing around a parent. Perhaps the parent appears too tired to say no. Maybe the kid appears spoiled or entitled.

But underneath, there's much more going on.

This book will take you on a journey of self-discovery. Along the way, you'll come face to face with the fears and insecurities that affect your parenting choices. You'll begin to recognize old, ineffective parenting methods and forge new ones that are right for your family and child. You'll learn why you became a bullied parent, and how to stop it once and for all.

My Own Journey

Before we get down to the nitty-gritty about bullied parents, I think it's best that I make a confession:

I was a bullied parent.

Yes, it's true. Like you, I stumbled into parenting with the best intentions—open-hearted and naïve. I was going to be the best parent I could be. I was going to out-parent my own parents. I was going to show the whole world what amazing children I could produce. *(That's right, me!)* After all, I am a psychotherapist who works with kids and families. Who's better prepared to be a parent than I?

Boy, did I have a lot to learn.

By the time my first daughter was six years old and my second was crawling around our home, I was stumbling about in a sleep-deprived haze, exhausted, brooding, and longing for my old life.

My oldest daughter's behavior dismayed and saddened me. She was rude, demanding, and mean; she spoke to me in ways that I would never have dared to speak to my parents. And yet whenever I tried to remedy the situation, I only made it worse.

I wasn't raising a well-adjusted child, but a first-class bully.

Soon, I found myself dodging conflicts with her. I couldn't take another meltdown or temper tantrum, particularly in public, where an audience seemed to boost her bullying powers. So, for a moment of peace I would give in to her demands. But those moments of peace were becoming shorter and shorter.

Why did she talk to me in such disrespectful ways?

Questions haunted and poked at me as I tossed and turned in bed at night:

Where did I go wrong?

Why am I afraid of her?

Am I being too permissive?

The one thing that I did know: whatever I was doing, it wasn't working.

A Turning Point

Every New Year's Day, I attend a celebration at the Buddhist center in my neighborhood. One of my favorite gatherings, it's filled with music, dancing, art, and poetry. Children giggle and run through the halls, old friends discover one another, hugs and kisses abound. What better way to start the New Year?

When it's time to leave, however, my daughter decides she wants to stay. She dashes away into the crowd, her arms flailing and hands waving as she darts between legs and under tables. "I don't want to go home, Papa!" she shrieks. "Leave me alone!"

I'm trying to stay calm, but inside I'm boiling. I have the creeping awareness that I'm being scrutinized. I begin to feel dizzy. My head throbs. *Get me the hell out of here*, I think. I receive a few sympatric looks from other parents—the ones who know my struggle. Members of the SPC (Suffering Parent Club) have an immediate identification—and an instant empathy—with one another. (Whenever I pass a father with a screaming kid in a stroller, I know exactly what he's going through. Immediately, our eyes meet and we share a silent exchange. *"I feel your pain, brother." "Thank you, brother."* And we go our separate ways.)

Back to my screaming, flailing daughter: It's the judgmental stares of nonparents that cut me to the quick. What the heck do they know about the challenges of being a parent? They live in a world of quiet dinners and sleep-filled nights, while I live in a prison crammed full of stuffed animals, princess dresses, and glitter.

As I chased my daughter around the Buddhist center, I felt my temperature rising. Here I am, a therapist who works with children, who leads parenting workshops, publishes parenting articles—and I don't have a clue what to do with my own kid!

As the eyes of others bore into me, a phrase of my father's springs from my lips, charged with menace and threat.

"Enough is enough!"

I scoop her up and head for the exit; she wiggles like a greased monkey in my arms. Once I find my car, I strap her into her car seat and slam the car door.

I think about how this must look like a kidnapping.

While driving home, all I can think about is revenge. Payback and punishments are the order of the day, and it's an order I can't wait to fill. I'll show her who's the boss.

I'm going to take away her stuffed animals and her favorite pillow.

I'll take away her bed, her bedroom door, and her mattress.

She'll be living in a prison cell begging me for forgiveness!

Just then my daughter grounds my flight of fantasy.

"Papa, why are you so mad?"

I'm stunned by the question. "Why am I so mad?" I sputter and puff. Her sincerity immobilizes me. Before I can respond, she states what is obvious to her, but not to me: "This is a happy day, Papa. You're making it a sad one."

I fumble for a defense. Deep down, I have the uncomfortable feeling that she's right. I'm acting out in ways that violate all my advice to parents. I'm vindictive, mean, and—worst of all—humorless. I feel like a complete failure. In the heat of the moment, all of my strategies, my training, schooling, and degrees: useless. What good is scholarly dissertation or self-help advice when my own parenting springs from such a low state of life?

When we arrive at home, I collapse in a chair and my eyes fall upon the parenting books that stock my bookshelves. I consider opening a window and tossing them out, one at a time. I imagine all the authors strolling down the street below my window. The books I hurl hit them in their heads with a delicious thump, and they collapse on the sidewalk.

Why had my training failed me?

Starting Over

After weeks of self-reflection and deep contemplation, I came to a painful realization: I had to jump off the blame train. Any satisfaction from blame was short-lived and left me feeling hopeless and bitter. Worse, the empty calories of blame made me a martyr, forever broadcasting my victimhood to the world. It was time to take responsibility for my daughter's behavior. After all, I am her parent. I raised her, didn't I? She came into the world with certain personality traits and temperaments, but ultimately, I must take responsibility for how she behaves.

In business, when a company falters, management comes under scrutiny. It's no different with parenting.

My daughter had every right to bully. She's a kid, and that's what kids do. The problem was my reaction to her bullying.

Rather than helping her manage her feelings and impulses, I was busy blaming her and trying to control her. Worse, I was responding to her bullying with my own bullying. When she got mad, I got madder. Instead of trying to understand her, I oppressed her, which only brought out greater defiance and bullying.

As a parent, I wasn't leading. I was reacting.

To paraphrase Gandhi, I had to *be the change I wanted to see in my child*. If I wanted her to be more patient, I had to be more patient. If I wanted her to be less bullying, I had to be less bullying. If I wanted her to be more mindful, I had to lead the way.

It was time for me to ditch my textbook knowledge of child psychology, my analytic training and psychobabble. My only escape from the Suffering Parent Club was to dig deep into my own past and uncover why I allowed my daughter to bully me.

Self-help advice without self-knowledge is rarely effective. It was time to stop blaming my child and take a good look in the mirror.

The New Deal

After a grueling period of self-analysis and introspection, I had a revelation. Actually, I had three:

1. My kid's behavior was a reflection of my own. If I wanted her to change her ways, I had to change mine.

2. My personal history—everything that made me *me*—lived and breathed in my parenting. I had to recognize and address the fears or insecurities that constantly influenced my parenting choices and allowed my daughter's bullying to flourish.

3. Learning to better manage my own feelings and impulses was central to turning around my relationship with my child and putting an end to bullying.

Purifying and understanding my internal world was the most important action I could take to improve my relationship with my daughter.

Parenting: The Ultimate Private Practice

Lawyers practice law, doctors practice medicine, and mothers and fathers practice parenting. *Practice* is the key word. It indicates an ongoing process of learning. Being a parent is not an identity; it's a part of who you are. To be a better parent, you have to consider all aspects of yourself—everything that makes you *you*.

Parenting offers us the chance to grow, to close gaps in our own maturity and become more complete. We all have immaturities, and they come to the surface when we become parents. Parenting is a relationship like no other. But there's at least one way in which our relationship with our kids is no different from any other relationship in our lives: It takes practice to make it better.

The Pancake Cure

After I hit rock bottom with my daughter, I decided to seek professional advice. It was a tough pill to swallow, but I was at my wit's end. Picking up the phone and making an appointment was a great education in itself. It helped me recognize how difficult it can be for a parent to ask for help. It stirred up so many uncomfortable feelings in me.

Am I failing as a parent?

Why do I sound like my own father?

What kind of therapist can't manage his own kid?

Research and many phone calls led me to a well-known, respected parenting specialist. After waiting weeks for an appointment and recovering from sticker shock (don't ask how much it cost), I made my way to his wood-paneled office, prepared to devour sage advice from across his great mahogany desk.

He listened to my sad story, closing his eyes and nodding knowingly. When I finished, he didn't say a word. For a moment I thought that he'd fallen asleep.

But then he opened his eyes, folded his hands on his lap, and sighed knowingly. "Take your daughter to breakfast three times a week."

I waited for more.

"That's it?" I asked.

"Let her talk, listen very closely to what she has to say. No advice, no opinions or guidance, just listen. Do that for a week or two, and things will turn around."

He rose from his chair. "And remember," he said, "children have temper tantrums; parents do not."

What the hell did that mean?

Before I could shout, "Refund!" I was out of the office and back in my car, grumbling all the way home.

Was he serious?

Listening was going to fix everything?

And what was that crack about temper tantrums?

I would follow his advice—but my expectations were very low.

That weekend when I told my daughter we were going to breakfast together, she smiled broadly. I figured anything involving pancakes would get a green light, but this was different. She was *really* excited. She grabbed her fancy hat and her favorite stuffed animal, and she raced for the door.

"Bye, Momma! Papa and I are going to breakfast!" she shouted cheerfully.

Once in our local diner, she chatted on and on about her favorite cartoons and movies, her last play date, and her special new friend at school. In the midst of it all, I began to realize how much she enjoyed having my full attention. She positively glowed. I tried not to talk, except to ask questions. She loved that even more.

We were sitting in a booth next to the window, enjoying our pancakes, when a woman outside on the street looked in on us. At first glance, I thought she was trying to see what we were eating, but then realized she was fixing her makeup in the reflection of the glass. As she applied eyeliner, she flared her nostrils most unattractively. My daughter giggled. "Look Papa. She's making a silly face."

We enjoyed a hearty laugh. A small moment perhaps, but for me, it was monumental. We were enjoying each other's company for the first time in a very long while.

That moment, and the breakfasts that followed, marked a turning point in our relationship, a start of an entirely new way of being together. I felt close to her, enjoyed her more. I began to ask myself what fears and insecurities caused her bullying behavior.

Then I recalled a conversation we had a few days after her sister arrived home. My daughter, clearly irritated, took me aside and whispered heatedly: "When's the baby going back to the hospital?"

I thought that she was joking. "The baby is staying with us," I assured her. "We're keeping her."

Her eyes widened and she put her hands on her hips. "You mean . . . like . . . forever?"

It had been right in front of me the whole time: The birth of her baby sister had rocked her world and pushed her out of the spotlight. She felt replaced by the new baby, and she didn't like it one bit.

Bullying was her way of expressing her upset. She felt discarded, tossed aside, and abandoned while we pampered and cooed over the new baby.

She wasn't feeling loved, she was feeling ignored. When children experience this kind of emotional neglect from their parents, it triggers profound fears of abandonment that can become a driving force of bullying behaviors.

No fear is more devastating to children than the loss of their parents' love; nothing undermines their sense of security quicker or destabilizes their emotional core faster.

Armed with my new understanding of her anxieties and my determination not to react to her bullying, I set out to make things right.

The next time she bullied, I hit the pause button. Rather than react, I asked myself:

What feelings have been stirred up in her?

Why is she bullying at this moment?

What's driving this behavior?

Rather than admonish her, I poured all my energy into trying to understand her and become empathically attuned to her feelings.

Make no mistake. This did not come naturally. It took enormous energy not to become reactive and escalate her bullying; it was the first in many battles for self-mastery.

I took a moment to collect my thoughts and asked calmly: "What's really bothering you? I can see it in your face. What is it?"

She looked away, tears of frustration forming in her eyes.

"Please tell me," I said. "I want to know. If you don't tell me, I won't know what's the matter. I want to help."

Finally, after a few aborted attempts, she blurted out, "You love . . . (sob) . . . the baby . . . (sob) more than me!" And she burst into tears.

"Is that what you think?" I asked her.

She nodded and buried her face in my shoulder, crying and gasping for air in the way that always breaks a parent's heart.

When my response to her bullying changed, she changed. Our mornings together paved the way, helped her feel loved and valued again. Once she felt understood, instead of expressing her upset through bullying, she was able to tell me directly in words what was bothering her.

Responding to her bullying with love and compassion changed everything. The more understood and accepted she felt, the more stable she became. Soon, there was no need to bully anymore.

How to Use This Book

All the tools in this book, all the parenting advice and guidance that you will find in the following chapters, are culled from my own experience as a parent, in addition to twenty years as a psychotherapist working with parents and children. I've done my best to identify the universal challenges that bullied parents face.

Many mothers and fathers look back on their early parenting with regret.

"I wish I knew then what I know now."

Rather than wishing to go back, let's go forward together.

The shortcut to a better understanding of your son or daughter begins with a better understanding of *you*. Your own childhood experiences, your thoughts and feelings, your impulses and actions, are all pieces of the bullied parent puzzle.

Throughout this journey, we're going to poke around your past for clues.

> ➤ How did you feel about your parents when you were your child's age?

> ➤ What did your parents do well and what didn't they do well?

> ➤ What specific memories come to mind when your kid is bullying you?

History shapes parenting. The solutions you seek to end bullying do not come from trying to control your kid. They come from self-mastery and mindfulness.

In this book, I don't suggest anything to you that I haven't employed myself, I make no recommendation that I haven't applied to my own parenting.

Freeing yourself from the prison of bullied parenthood is hard work; it won't happen overnight. But with each breakthrough moment, you'll gain greater freedom and a deeper understanding of yourself and your son or daughter. You may be surprised to discover how similar you are.

Getting Started

To win the battle of the bully, you'll need to develop a new level of consciousness. Conscious and unconscious emotional baggage from your past—esteem problems, resentments, shames, fears and anxieties, self-neglecting habits, narcissistic tendencies, and resistances to closeness—are plunked down in the space between you and your child. To put energy into changing your kid without considering your own history is like trying to change a shadow on a wall without altering the object casting it.

Before we get started, let's take a sneak peak of what's to come in the following chapters.

Chapter Two: What Happened to My Sweet, Adorable Child?

In Chapter 2, we'll examine the interplay between two powerful forces: your child's emotional development and how it interacts with your history.

We'll begin with a primer on child development, followed by a quick review of the unique challenges that each developmental stage presents. Each stage includes a test period in which children challenge their parents' authority. How parents manage these test periods often determines whether their children will become bullies.

We'll consider four developmental stages:

1. Early childhood and preschool

2. Small children and toddlers

3. School age and preteen

4. Teen and young adult

We'll wrap up with a list of immediate steps, as well as the long-term interventions you can take to address bullying behaviors at home.

Chapter Three: How We Become Our Kids' Victims— and Strategies to Prevent Parent Burnout

Here, we'll begin to understand how your personal insecurities may be undermining your parenting and eroding your leadership. We look at the histories of parents who are most likely to be bullied:

➤ Parents who were bullied by their own parents

> Parents who had absent or neglectful parents

> Parents who had narcissistic parents

We'll explore how self-neglect may be undoing your effectiveness as a parent and fueling your kid's bullying. We'll finish with the *Parent's Burnout Prevention Checklist* so that you can regain the energy and confidence you'll need to stand up to your child's bullying and provide the leadership all kids crave from their parents.

Chapter Four: Understanding Your Kid's Bullying Behavior Style

In Chapter 4, we'll learn what makes bullies tick. We'll look at the three most common bullying styles:

1. The defiant bully

2. The anxious bully

3. The manipulative bully

As we walk through the unique behavior of each bullying style, we'll take a closer look at the unconscious forces that generate those bullying behaviors. By grasping those forces, we can begin to differentiate what our children want from what they need.

Next, we'll step into households with bullies and see how their behavior impacts the entire family. We'll see how the parents' personalities and histories intertwine with their child's bullying style and temperament. Each scenario will conclude with recommendations and a peek inside my office to discover the strategies that parents use to end bullying and restore balance to their families.

Chapter Five: Your Parenting Style— and How Good Parents Fall into Bad Habits

Next, we'll turn our attention to bullied parents and gain a deeper understanding of why they allow their kids to bully them. We'll look at the three parenting styles that are most likely to provoke bullying in children:

1. The guilty parent

2. The anxious parent

3. The fix-everything parent

Through examples and real-life scenarios, we'll come to see the complexities of bullying and how good parents fall into bad habits. We'll uncover the universal struggles of bullied parents and discover how lasting solutions come from greater mindfulness.

Chapter Six: Tools to Give You Both Just the Right Amount of Power

In Chapter 6, I'll help you design a personalized parenting toolbox based on your own unique identity and history. I'll share with you three guidelines for strengthening your confidence and remaining steadfast in ending bullying behaviors:

1. Stick to your vision.

2. Take responsibility for your behavior.

3. Manage your feelings.

Each tool will spring from a greater self-understanding. Each will enable you to make better choices in heated moments. Together, we'll design specific responses to your child's particular style of bullying.

Chapter Seven: How to Assemble Your Anti-Bullying Support Team

Putting an end to bullying in your household will require that you gather the right support. In Chapter 7, you'll learn how to assemble an anti-bullying team. We'll explore four key steps to strengthen your parenting:

1. Uniting with your partner or spouse

2. Enlisting your friends

3. Involving school officials

4. Talking to mental health professionals

Too often, bullied parents isolate themselves or feel ashamed of their situation. Involving others is a key step in strengthening your resolve and ending bullying once and for all.

Chapter Eight: Navigating the Seven Parenting Crises That Can Trigger Bullying

Sometimes bullying behaviors emerge slowly, over a long period of time; sometimes they seem to appear overnight. Many are triggered by disruptive events that destabilize children.

We'll look at *Seven Parenting Crises* most common in families and how they have the potential to produce bullying:

1. Illness and injury

2. Trauma

3. Divorce

4. Adoption

5. Financial hardship

6. Learning issues

7. Death

This chapter will prime you to lead your family through these challenging situations while helping your kid develop greater emotional resilience and stop relying on bullying for stress relief.

The Parent Power Notebook

You may be wondering: How are we going to initiate your parenting revolution?

Many parents find that keeping a parenting journal is instrumental in helping them break free of old patterns and open up new pathways in parenting. A journal forces you to make time for self-reflection and deeper consideration of your choices as a parent. Most important, a journal can be instrumental in helping you break reactive habits that escalate conflicts and fuel bullying behaviors.

In this journal, you'll be encouraged to jot down thoughts, feelings, and memories; you'll begin to mine your past for the origins to problems in your relationship with your child. You'll also be asked to set goals and record your breakthroughs.

Writing goals will help you keep focused, especially when you start to feel adrift. Goals are like compasses—handy when you feel lost. Goals will also keep you anchored during stormy times and remind you to stay on course.

What you decide to call your journal is up to you. Many parents refer to it as "My Parent Power Notebook." One divorced dad called it "My Mad-as-Hell Rants." A single mom named it, "Art's Way" after her favorite uncle. She would often say, "I'm going to spend time with Uncle Art," before setting off to write in her journal.

No doubt for some of you, the idea of a journal will be met with resistance.

"I don't have time to keep a journal."

It's true that parents are busy. But the time you put into your journal will pay off in countless ways. It will bring more mindfulness to your parenting, lead to greater insight into your son's or daughter's issues, and empower you to reduce bullying by diminishing conflicts.

"I'm not a journal person."

Okay, maybe the idea of a journal is hokey to you. I get it. So, just mull over the questions and jot down responses on a notepad or in the margins of this book. The important thing is that you begin to consider your parenting in a new light.

"This doesn't feel natural. Why do I have to work this hard?"

What I ask of you in the coming chapters *will not feel natural.* To master any new skill requires practice. Becoming an effective parent is no different.

The journal is an essential tool for personal development, self-renewal, and empowerment. And most important, it will serve as your personal guide out of the world of the bullied parent!

Journaling Tips

Set aside time in your day when you have a quiet moment to yourself. For many parents, early-morning journaling is best, before the sun rises and your kids shatter the fragile peace in your home. Do what you can to carve out some quality journaling time when you are alone or when your kid is at school or at a friend's house.

Parents tend to get caught in reactive loops—wiping up spills, settling arguments, packing lunch boxes, or sending off college tuition payments—tending to task after task, crisis after crisis. Too often, rather than being proactive and making mindful decisions and choices, bullied parents become reactive, mindlessly servicing their kids and working themselves into a state of never-ending exhaustion. And here's the worst part: The more like that you are, the more your kid will bully you.

Getting Started with Your Parenting Journal

Once you've set aside some time for yourself, ditch all technology. That's right, turn off your cell phone, Internet, MP3 player. Minimize distractions. Strengthening your parenting begins with strengthening mindfulness. A commitment to journaling is a commitment to building a solid emotional core so you can face down your insecurities and stand up to your·child's bullying.

Once you start writing, don't stop. Don't think too much, don't backtrack or edit. Keep pushing forward.

Ready? Here we go.

What are the top three power struggles you have with your kid?

_____.

_____.

_____.

What triggers your kid's bullying?

_____

_____.

My kid tends to bully most when _____.

_____ *is the worst*

time of day for my kid.

My kid starts to bully whenever we discuss _____

_____.

Do you behave in ways that make bullying worse?

I escalate conflicts when I _____.

I always regret when I _____.

My kid gets most enraged when I _____.

chapter two

What happened to my sweet, adorable child?

t happens all the time. Parents arrive in my office in a state of shock, wondering how their sweet, adorable child morphed into a domestic tyrant.

To gain a better understanding of the origins of this bullying behavior, let's look at some basic child psychology and see how developmental phases come with built-in power struggles and test periods that have the potential to turn into bullying.

Little Monster Psych. 101

In each developmental phrase, children wrestle with new skills and abilities. Learning to walk, use language, or write—these are mighty struggles for little folk.

If a phase goes well, after a period of intense struggle and sustained effort, a breakthrough finally occurs. The breakthrough comes in the form of a personal victory that changes everything. In an amazingly short period of time, the child discards his old way of doing things and determines to keep moving forward. For example:

> The baby who has just fed himself with a spoon no longer wants to be fed.

> The wobbly child who just learned to walk has no further interest in crawling.

> The teenager who has just gotten his driver's license abandons his bike in the garage.

Each time your kid masters a new skill, he makes a leap in maturity. He loves the feeling of mastery and experiences a rush of joy and confidence in his own abilities. He is stronger and more powerful.

And of course, when children reach these personal milestones, their parents are their clamorous cheerleaders. Kids soak up parental applause and admiration; it motivates them to keep striving for greater mastery.

Here things start to get a little more complicated.

The Drive for Independence Promotes Conflict

With mastery comes a yearning for greater independence. In other words, kids will begin to reject their parents' support. For example:

> The baby who has learned to feed herself forcefully pushes her parent's hand away.

> The toddler who has learned to walk cries out when his parents try to assist him.

> The teenager with the driver's license doesn't want his parents in the car.

Inexperience and impulsivity complicate a child's drive for greater independence. Children don't know their limits; they don't know when to stop and when to go, they don't always know what's good for them and what's not. One thing they do know, however: they don't want their parents hovering over them.

Since no kid is prepared to live without adult supervision, eventually every parent has the unpopular job of going against her kid's will. It's impossible to be a good parent without saying no from time to time.

Here is where the battle of wills begins.

How Frustration Gives Way to Bullying

As a rule, children don't like hearing the word no, especially from their parents. The moment parents prevent their kids from getting what they want, kids are perplexed.

Why are my parents ruining my fun?

Can't they see I'm enjoying myself?

Why are they getting in my way?

They don't understand that their parents are protecting them. It feels like restraint, and they don't like it.

The Bully Impulse

It's human nature to rebel against restrictions. No kids want a parent standing between them and what they want. In other words, nature puts kids and their parents on a collision course. That's why, eventually, all healthy children must enter into battle with their parents.

This fight is natural and *necessary*. It's how children can begin to define themselves as different from their parents. They have their own wants and needs, their own interests. If children are too accommodating or too compliant with their parents, they will lack confidence and self-definition in life.

In every developmental phase, children instinctively battle against their parents' restrictions.

> ➤ The small child fights her parents as they strap her in her stroller.

> ➤ The toddler runs away from his parents at bedtime.

> ➤ The teenager brawls with her parents over chores and curfews.

As parents impose their will on their kids, sparks fly. These clashes are an unavoidable and important part of parenting. Every good parent eventually scuffles with his kid in a battle of youthful rebellion.

Testing Moments

After parents set a restriction, we enter into a crucial moment. The child begins to test how far he can push his parents to give him what he wants. It's his will against theirs. The old-fashioned standoff commences. The kid thinks:

If I scream for it, will dad give in?

If I cry, will I get my way?

If I make a scene, will mom surrender?

It's impossible to look away from a testing moment when it happens in public. You wonder to yourself:

Who will back down first?

Who will win this battle?

Who will compromise?

When parents stay firm, refuse to concede, or give in to demands, many kids will push the conflict to another level.

Here we reach a tipping point.

When Testing Turns to Bullying

From preschool to high school, test periods are the prime clashing points in all parent–child relationships. They are trying times, when kids flex their young muscles and test their parents' tenacity.

When your kid begins to bully you, do you…

> ➤ Surrender and give him what he wants?

> ➤ Hold your ground?

> ➤ Bully back?

Okay, let's pause here and take a moment to remember that parents are human. They have good days and bad days. On good days, they are good-humored and flexible, and they have boundless patience—or at least enough patience. On bad days, they are grumpy; they lose their temper and sometimes act like children themselves.

As kids battle their parents, parents do battle with themselves.

Do I surrender?

Do I punish?

Do I negotiate?

How important are these test periods? How you manage them ultimately determines whether your child will become your bully.

Let's examine a typical testing moment and consider the three most common parenting responses.

Three Common Tactics That Fall Short

It's the end of a long day. You've just arrived home from work, completely pooped. You flip on the TV, collapse on the sofa, and catch the end of your favorite program. You savor this quiet time.

Just then, your kid begins to whine and carry on. He wants a slice of chocolate cake before dinner. You tell him no.

"You promised!" he demands. "You said I could have it when you got home."

You tell him to wait until after dinner. He stands in front of the TV. "I want it now. Right now!"

You close your eyes and take a breath. Maybe you count to ten. But your kid turns up the volume: "You lied to me! I waited all day for you! I hate you! You're stupid!"

Okay, freeze-frame! This testing moment has just tipped into a bullying moment. You're being verbally assaulted and degraded by your own child.

What do you do?

Typically, parents choose one of three responses in such moments: *surrender, punish,* or *negotiate.*

Surrender

Not every battle is worth fighting; surrendering and giving your kid what he wants is *sometimes* a good option—especially if you're looking to buy yourself a bit of peace.

But when testing turns into bullying—*never* give in to your child's demands. To do so would be tantamount to rewarding abusive behavior. It's a teaching moment that delivers the wrong lesson!

Every time you surrender to your kid's bullying, you send her this simple message: *Bullying works.* So the next time she's frustrated by your restrictions, she will bully to get what she wants; after all, you have taught her that if she pushes hard enough, you'll surrender.

Punish

When your kid bullies you, it's difficult not to become reactive and bully back. Possessing the strength of character to resist mirroring your kid's aggressive behavior is a skill that rarely comes naturally to parents. Like any form of self-mastery, it must be cultivated.

Losing your cool, hollering, and coming down on your kid with harsh punishments are forms of counter-bullying that create a culture of bullying in the family.

Parents who win battles with their kids by leaning heavily on punishment achieve a bitter victory. In this scenario, there's a winner and a loser. Someone is happy and someone isn't.

Children who are constantly punished become contemptuous and resentful. Once this occurs, more serious behavior problems will emerge. For example, kids:

> ➤ Become defiant and oppositional, directly or through silent resistance.

> ➤ Turn their frustration inward and fall victim to depression or anxiety.

> ➤ Bully more intensely, escalating conflicts and disrupting the entire family.

Negotiate

Okay, your kid is having a meltdown. Being a mindful parent, you take a moment and consider your options. You try to understand your kid's perspective: He waited all day for you and for his cake. Then, when you finally got home, instead of greeting him, you collapsed on the couch, turned on the TV, and ignored him.

You get it. He's upset, and he has a right to be. So you decide to cut a deal. You offer half a slice of cake now, and the other half after dinner.

> ➤ Is negotiation the best choice in this moment?

> ➤ What if he makes a counteroffer?

> ➤ Suppose he continues to bully and demands the whole slice?

Negotiation is a popular choice in modern parenting. The notion of finding common ground with your kid during conflicts is not a bad idea. You give a little, he gives a little, and everyone is happy. Right?

Yes and no.

When testing turns to bullying, negotiation is off the table. When you negotiate with a bully, you set the stage for ongoing conflicts. Like surrendering, it rewards bullying and trains your kid that bullying works. The next time your kid is frustrated by your restrictions, he will return to bullying because bullying leads to negotiation, and negotiation leans to getting what he wants.

Another flaw with negotiation: Kids might begin to think that everything, even good behavior, is negotiable. Rather than doing something for themselves and the good feelings it produces, they do it to get a reward. For example:

> ➤ Your daughter demands to get paid for making her bed.

> ➤ Your son expects a reward for doing his homework.

> ➤ Your kids ask for cash for good grades.

Good behavior should never be a bartering point. Negotiating for rewards replaces the personal achievement—and kids miss out on esteem. Rather than developing self-reliance and autonomy, they remain immature and tethered to their parents for gratification.

Immediate Steps You Can Take

You just learned that surrendering, punishing, and negotiating all fall short in the long run. These tactics offer some short-term relief by managing the symptoms of bullying, but don't address its causes.

Before we look at the deeper issues, let's consider the three most important steps you can take in bullying moments: *de-escalate the conflict*, *validate feelings*, and *praise strengths*.

1. De-escalate the Conflict

In bullying moments, parents too often react impulsively and escalate conflicts. They yell or punish, which increases the tension and worsens the bullying. It's vital for you to maintain your composure and leadership in such moments. Don't become reactive or fall back on knee-jerk responses. Stand your ground without drama.

If the conflict escalates, hit the pause button: Take a time out and give everyone a chance to cool off. When kids are in a state of intense frustration, you can't reason with them. In fact, if you try, you'll only increase their frustration.

You and your kid will benefit greatly from a quiet moment to gather your thoughts and regain your equilibrium. If you can, leave the room or take a quiet walk. Get some fresh air. It will give you both time to calm down. Find some peace in yourself before you try to make peace with your kid. Then, once things have quieted down, you can mindfully consider what actions to take.

2. Validate Feelings

You can never go wrong by validating your kid's feelings.

"I understand that you're frustrated. I am, too."

"I can see you're upset. Give me ten minutes of quiet to think about this."

"Let's have something to eat first. We'll both feel better."

Kids respond positively when their feelings are acknowledged. They immediately start to calm down.

During the break, ask yourself: "What could be causing my kid's bullying? Is he tired? Hungry? Feeling neglected? Has it been a long day for everyone? Maybe he's spent too long playing a computer game or surfing the net?"

Bullying is an effect; there's always an underlying cause. Consider what could be making your kid so irritable. Help him speak his mind, and validate his feelings.

"I understand that you're angry; you have a right to be."

"Your feelings are hurt. You're mad that I won't give you what you want."

"Instead of fighting, let's try something new. Tell me why you're so mad."

Encourage more mature communication. Feeling understood by you will defuse his frustration and reframe the moment.

Remember: Give kids what they need, not what they want. Learning to communicate effectively while frustrated is more important than anything that your kid is craving in the moment. Surrendering, punishing, or negotiating robs kids of the opportunity to wrestle with frustration and master it. Make it clear that bullying never works.

"I'm not going to respond as long as you're yelling at me."

"Bullying is not going to get you what you want."

"You can do better than this. You're too smart to be a bully."

3. Praise Progress

Once a decision is reached, stand your ground. Don't revisit it lest your kid tests you and pushes for more. Along the way, be sure to praise your kid's strengths.

"I appreciate how you are talking to me right now."

"I know this was hard for you. I'm proud of the way you expressed yourself."

"You're doing a great job. You're really maturing."

Reinforcing your kid's strengths will boost his confidence and make mature communication more rewarding than bullying.

The Pancake Cure Revisited

Even though our weekly breakfasts dramatically improved my relationship with my daughter, there was still work to be done.

In many ways, it would have been easier to give in, punish, or negotiate with her. But none of those choices would have addressed her underlying feelings. Let's apply the three steps to her bullying moment and see how it changed the outcome.

When I remained calm in the face of her upset, it de-escalated the tension. I took a moment to consider why she was acting up. I asked myself, what were the possible causes of her irritation? Knowing she was upset about all the attention her new baby sister was getting, I managed to shift the conversation to a new, more mature level.

Validating her feelings had a calming effect on her. By giving her all my attention and doing my best to understand her, I was able to help her express her deeper upset—she was feeling neglected and unloved—and verbalize her insecurities. Putting her frustration into words, wrestling with self-expression, had a maturing effect on her.

In other words, she was able to transcend her bullying impulse and express the hurt behind it. If I had surrendered, punished, or negotiated, I would have resolved her frustration but denied her the opportunity for emotional growth.

Frustration is the fossil fuel for maturity. When we empower kids to manage their frustration and express it maturely, bullying becomes less gratifying to them.

Long-Term Steps You Can Take to Cure Bullying

Okay, you've resolved your kid's bullying, for now; you've put an end to the immediate conflict. Still, a bigger question looms: Why is your son or daughter bullying you in the first place?

Remember, bullying is a symptom of deeper issues, the effect of hidden causes. The first step in getting to the root of it is to make a quick assessment of your kid's lifestyle.

Chances are, there is something missing from your child's life. To neutralize bullying behavior and prevent it from worsening, let's address what could be missing in the context of the following five basic requirements for healthy social and emotional development. (This checklist is wildly popular in my parenting workshops.)

REQUIREMENTS FOR KIDS' HEALTHY SOCIAL AND EMOTIONAL DEVELOPMENT

❑ *Find tension outlets.*

❑ *Build self-esteem.*

❑ *Set structure, limits, and boundaries.*

❑ *Seek out great teachers, models, and mentors.*

❑ *Use learning diagnostics.*

1. Find Tension Outlets

Studies have shown that thirty minutes of cardio exercise, three or more times a week, reduces anxious/depressive symptoms up to 70 percent. Seventy percent!

Exercise produces endorphins, the "feel-good" chemicals of the brain, which help lower anxiety and depression—two big causes of bullying. Kids who have regular tension outlets feel better, think more clearly, and sleep more soundly after workouts because they discharge stress stored in their bodies. Exercise also increases kids' metabolism by getting their hearts racing and pumping fresh oxygen into their blood.

Kids who have healthy tension outlets feel better about themselves. They're less interested in bullying or mistreating their parents.

The idea of exercise may conjure up images of grueling aerobic classes or punishing sessions with a personal trainer. Perhaps you are thinking: "How on earth am I supposed to get my kid to go to the gym?"

Anything that gets your kid's body moving is a step in the right direction. Start wherever you can. If sports teams are out of the question, there are plenty of noncompetitive forms of exercise such as swimming, biking, hiking, dancing, yoga, tai chi, or martial arts. You can even start by taking walks together.

When a young person enters my office, I can tell right away through his body language and his mood whether or not tension outlets are a part of his life. Kids without tension outlets are more rigid and inflexible, physically and emotionally. You can see the stress stored in their bodies—stress that they often discharge through bullying their parents.

TERRY THE GAMER

The moment Terry arrived home from school, he'd log on to his favorite gaming site and play for hours. Afterward, his mood was worse than when he started. Cranky and short tempered, he bullied his mother without remorse, refusing to do chores, do homework, or even shower.

The effect of computer games on a kid's mood depends on his temperament and activity level. If your kid has plenty of friends, cardio workouts and positive creative outlets, games won't likely affect his mood. But if your kid has none of those things and spends all his time gaming, you're in for trouble.

No one benefits from countless hours of gaming except game manufacturers. In fact, many games actually increase players' tension and stress levels. And if there's no physical outlet, bullying their parents can become the primary method of tension relief.

The more kids disappear into the world of the game, the less interest or patience they have for the world of the living.

Add to that the infatuation with immediate gratification, social isolation, and a decrease in personal ambition, and gamers begin to look a lot like addicts.

Terry the Gamer absolutely refused to exercise, and by tenth grade he was borderline obese. Besides being unhealthy, his weight had a terrible effect on his self-esteem and peer relationships.

After I met for several sessions with Terry's parents, they agreed it was time to limit gaming. They told him that in order to continue gaming, he'd have to get moving. Exercise was no longer optional.

After a few failed attempts, Terry's dad (who also struggled with his weight) began to take walks with Terry after dinner. At first, these walks were in silence, with Terry grudgingly following far behind. Slowly, however, he began to talk about his struggles in school, which he usually kept secret. As his father listened, he validated Terry's feelings by sharing his own difficulties from high school.

Terry began to feel much closer to his father. He felt understood and validated. Taking time walking together helped de-escalate conflicts, discharge tension, and reboot Terry's relationship with his dad.

Terry's father recalls: "At first I thought, 'How is walking together going to help?' Then I started to notice changes in Terry's mood. He was happier, more cooperative. One night, after dinner, he actually said to me, 'Hey dad, let's leave early. I want to add a few more blocks tonight.'"

The real breakthrough came when Terry expressed interest in taking fencing classes. Fencing's language of combat—assault and attack—sounded a lot like the video games he loved. After a shaky introductory class, Terry began to get the hang of it. He even asked his parents if he could sign up for more classes.

When Terry's coach, who'd quickly become an important mentor, suggested that he begin to spar in matches, to everyone's surprise, Terry agreed.

In a short time, Terry's mood improved and his sense of humor was back. None of this would have happened if his parents hadn't taken a stand. They gave Terry what he needed (tension outlets) rather than what he wanted (more gaming time).

In a matter of weeks, Terry's bullying was no longer an issue. He felt better about himself and, as a result, was better to his parents.

2. Build Self-Esteem

Every kid needs three to five sources of self-esteem—activities, talents, or hobbies that produce a feeling of personal pride. Without diverse sources of self-esteem, kids are more likely to engage in bullying behaviors.

All bullies struggle with esteem issues. That's why it's crucial for you to help your kid to scope out and develop unique talents, skills, and passions. If your child has only one source of self-esteem, he is less insulated against life's tribulations. The moment he fails at that particular thing, his esteem will collapse. No kid's entire sense of self-worth should come from one source. Children who have numerous sources of esteem bully less and manage life's ups and downs better.

When it comes to activities that produce self-esteem, look for anything that your child expresses an interest in, whether it's sports, photography, art, music, design, or another activity. If she doesn't express an interest in anything, you're going to have to shop around until something clicks. If she says no, it doesn't mean that you're off the hook. Be firm, take the lead, and keep exploring options!

MEET SPIRITED STEPHANIE

Stephanie, a middle-schooler, was a real challenge for her teachers. She had difficulty staying in her seat; she was constantly up and down, chatting, and moving around the classroom. When her teacher put limits on her behaviors, Stephanie became disruptive and whiny.

Stephanie's chaotic energy exhausted her parents, too. They'd tried everything—surrender, punishment, and negotiation. They'd hung behavior charts in her room and on their refrigerator door, rewarding her with stickers for good behavior. They'd even enrolled her in a behavior modification program. But nothing seemed to help.

The solution, however, was hiding in plain sight.

Stephanie loved to watch dance performances. She would spend hours in front of the TV watching dance competitions. Whether hip-hop, modern, ballroom, ballet, tap, or jazz—it didn't matter. If it was dance, Stephanie was interested. She could sit quietly watching for hours, often getting up and imitating the dancers' moves.

A guidance counselor suggested that Stephanie enroll in a dance class at the local youth center. She did, and it changed her life. Her mother recalls: "Watching Stephanie in her first class, I held my breath. I thought she would be her typical disruptive self. But she was a completely different child in that class. She couldn't stop smiling. She was well behaved, attentive. Afterward, I signed her up for three classes a week."

Once Stephanie found something that she loved, something she was proud of and gave her pride, everything changed. Dance gave her structure and a positive outlet for all her bottled-up energy. It fed her self-esteem. Stephanie did better academically and socially. And her dance teacher also served as a wonderful role model and mentor.

Bullying fills a void in a child's life. Give your kid something positive to do with her energy. Provide esteem-building activities, and you'll be amazed at how quickly bullying behaviors begin to fade away.

3. Set Structure, Limits, and Boundaries

Structure, limits, and boundaries are frameworks that parents provide to help foster healthy habits in their children. As kids internalize these structures, they develop an aptitude for organizing their thoughts, feelings, and impulses. They manage their time better, relate mindfully, and balance their wants with the needs of others. Positive structure, limits, and boundaries also help children develop better judgment and stronger moral fiber.

Here's the catch: Kids aren't born with these frameworks; parents must provide them. In the absence of healthy structure, limits, and boundaries, bullying behaviors are sure to emerge.

Let's take a look at the role that structure, limits, and boundaries play in preventing a bully from appearing in your home.

Structure Consistent schedules around bedtimes, dinner times, homework rituals, chores, and other activities are vital for lowering anxiety and reducing children's tension. These routines and tasks may seem monotonous, but for kids, they're indispensable. Structure imposes order on chaos. As an organizing force, it soothes angst. It helps kids take better care of themselves and their environments.

Limits Limits are restrictions that parents put on potentially destructive behaviors. The ultimate goal of limits is to insert a thoughtful pause between urge and action. Typically, kids who bully their parents never received enough behavioral limits, particularly during test periods when they saw how far they could push for what they wanted.

Limit setting is greatly influenced by parenting style, kids' temperaments, and family culture. Family culture accounts for vastly different expectations of children's behavior. Some families are stricter and lean heavily on respect and personal responsibility. In such a culture, bullying is rarely an issue. Other families are too permissive and fail to provide enough limits. In this type of culture, bullied parents are plentiful.

But striking a balance is crucial. Too many limits may crush a child's sense of exploration and wonder. Too few will keep him from developing mindfulness and self-respect.

Boundaries Boundaries concern the space between people and how you teach your kid to manage it. Bullies nearly always have poor boundaries. They don't know where they end and others begin. Consequently, they may invade personal space or manipulate others to get what they want.

Boundaries come in two forms: physical and emotional. Physical boundaries involve respecting physical space. Emotional boundaries involve respecting other people's feelings and communicating thoughtfully.

Poor structure, limits, and boundaries can breed bullying behaviors. Without structure, limits, and boundaries, kids grow impulsive and unmanageable.

Remember, the goal of these frameworks is not to change or control your kid, but to take the raw power of youth, with all its vitality and madcap energy, and give it a vessel for positive expression. For example, as your kid's interests and talents emerge, strive to find a structure for him, such as athletic activities, music, or dance—anything that can help develop his aptitudes and abilities. As he progresses toward mastery, bullying won't interest him. And these frameworks will enable him to develop two important skills: resilience and self-discipline.

MEET THE ENVIABLE EVIN

Evin loved to brag about the freedoms his parents gave him. He didn't have curfews or chores, he could stay out late, and his parents never involved themselves in his schoolwork. Evin could curse at his parents or yell at them with no consequences. He got away with saying things that most kids would never dream of saying to their parents.

Needless to say, many of his friends were consumed with envy. In their eyes, Evin had it all.

One day, when Evin was absent, the group discussed the freedoms his parents gave him. Group members imagined how happy they'd be if only they had parents like Evin's.

After much exploration I made them an offer: "How about I convince your parents to give you all the freedoms that Evin has?"

There was a unanimous guffaw.

"Yeah, right."

"Not going to happen."

"Good luck with that one."

The thought of their parents failing to provide structure, limits, and boundaries for them was outrageous. They accused me of living in a fantasy.

Just then, Susie, a precocious preteen, took the floor. "My parents would never let me live like Evin," she said.

"Why not?" I asked.

"Because my parents love me."

Parents often see the frameworks I have mentioned as negative, when, in fact, it's just the opposite. Without structure, limits, and boundaries, kids feel unloved.

4. Seek out Terrific Teachers, Models, and Mentors

Nothing is more powerful than an adult who can inspire and motivate your kid. An uplifting teacher, a cheering coach, a supportive aunt or uncle, or a popular family friend—these positive relationships have the power to make kids drop bullying behaviors overnight as they strive to be more like the adults that inspire them.

Think of the transformations that Terry and Stephanie went through when each discovered an activity that they loved. Both benefited from the cardio and esteem boost they experienced, but those activities also put them in contact with adults that they could look up to—mentors who inspired them to behave better.

The more a mentor believes in a kid, the more that kid believes in himself. A kid's future is brighter and his sense of purpose is stronger, when an inspiring adult takes an active interest and teaches him a better way of being.

When searching for models and mentors for your kid, it's best to find someone outside the immediate family's orbit. If your daughter talks lovingly about a favorite teacher, for example, let that teacher know how important she is to your kid.

5. Use Learning Diagnostics

Whenever I hear a bullied parent describe her kid as lazy or apathetic about schoolwork, I immediately become suspicious.

Why isn't her kid doing better in school?

What's really going on here?

The most likely cause is undiagnosed learning differences. In the old days, children were labeled "learning disabled" or "emotionally disturbed." But these kids weren't disabled or disturbed; they simply saw things differently. The labels were inaccurate and didn't benefit anyone.

Some kids have distinctive ways of processing information and difficulty learning in school, particularly in certain subjects. Their idiosyncratic ways of learning don't make them disabled, but unique. Understanding their learning styles and finding the combination to unlock their potential is key to helping them succeed academically.

When kids have learning styles that don't fit well with a school's approach, kids experience constant tension in the classroom. By the time they get home, they're exhausted, irritable, and likely to dump the stress of the day onto their parents.

Learning differences are more likely to appear in middle and high school, as schoolwork gets more challenging and reading, writing, and math assignments become more complicated.

When kids begin to fall short academically, their parents are often baffled. "What happened?" they wonder. "Why is my kid suddenly failing in school?"

As parents grow increasingly frustrated, they tend to put more pressure on their kids—who are already feeling pressured at school. So, now they are pressured at home, too? How much more pressure can they stand? Soon, communication breaks down and wars break out over homework, chores, and other responsibilities. In such cases, bullying is a natural outcome of living with too much stress.

Neuropsychological Evaluation When kids have a history of academic struggles, I always recommend a neuropsychological evaluation, or *neuro-psych*, for short. Psychologists in schools, mental health clinics, learning centers, and private practices can perform these evaluations. (For a complete list of mental health professions and their specialties, see *How to Assemble Your Anti-Bullying Support Team* in Chapter 7.)

Simply put, a neuro-psych measures cognitive performance. The evaluations usually take up to ten hours to complete, which can be spread over ten sessions. When the test is finished, parents are given a full picture of their child's learning style, strengths, and weaknesses, in addition to the effects of biological history, parenting, and temperament.

During the neuro-psych, the psychologist works one-on-one with the child, applying a series of tests to ascertain how the child processes information. For example, does the child have difficulty:

> Sustaining attention in certain subjects?

> Decoding symbols or reading?

> Putting thoughts down on paper?

The comprehensive test also includes measurements for auditory and visual functioning, processing speeds, motor skills, intelligence, memory, speech, and organizational skills.

The results are always enlightening. For example, many bullying kids score high on intellect functioning and reasoning and low on organizational skills or memory. This is like having a high-performance car that can only go fifteen miles an hour.

Once these learning differences are identified, academic accommodations are recommended to help the child succeed in school. The recommendations could include working with a learning specialist, extra time on exams, academic support in school, or specialized classroom instruction. Such accommodations can make a huge difference in a kid's academic performance and should be considered by any bullied parent whose child is struggling in school.

MEET HEARTBREAKING HENRY

Henry always did well in class; he sailed through elementary school with little effort.

Middle school, however, was an entirely different story.

From sixth to eighth grade, as Henry's grades tumbled, his mood at home began to deteriorate. He talked back to his parents, bullied them, and refused to complete assignments. Afternoon and evenings invariably erupted into battles over homework.

Henry's transformation from a good-hearted and friendly child to an unhappy bully was heartbreaking.

Henry's parents contacted me because the school guidance counselor thought Henry would benefit from therapy. After hearing Henry's history, I recommended a neuro-psych. Henry's parents were taken aback.

"He's just lazy."

"He's not working up to his potential."

"He doesn't apply himself."

Three months later, as Henry's bullying worsened, they finally agreed to the evaluation. The results were startling: Henry's scores in abstract reasoning and intelligence were off the charts; he was truly gifted. However, his auditory processing and executive functioning scores were low.

Henry's auditory delays limited his ability to process information at the same speeds as his classmates. It was nearly impossible for him to keep up with spoken instructions in class. His executive functioning—the ability to plan, initiate, and complete complex tasks—was also particularly weak for his intelligence. He needed a learning specialist to train him to better organize his notebooks and map out assignments.

Henry wasn't lazy or difficult. He was failing because his learning differences made it difficult to keep up with his class. Once he began using a word processor in class, working with a learning specialist on his homework, getting extra time on exams, and receiving academic support at school, Henry's grades began to improve. He felt better about himself, and his bullying behaviors vanished.

The Cost of an Evaluation One final note about neuro-psych evaluations: They can be very expensive. Public schools usually provide them for free. However, some schools don't have psychologists on staff or have a long waiting list for evaluations.

If your insurance company will cover a private evaluation, look for a psychologist who specializes in youth and ask to read one of that professional's complete evaluations. Be sure to choose someone with whom you and your kid are comfortable.

If your insurance company won't pay for a neuro-psych and you have a tight budget, many graduate schools or training institutes offer testing for free or at a discount. Students under the supervision of a licensed psychologist usually administer these tests.

Learning differences are among the top reasons for bullying behaviors. A good psychologist can help identify learning issues and get your kid the support and academic accommodations he needs in order to feel successful in school. But no single intervention will correct your bullying child's behaviors. To put an end to bullying, we need to consider the whole child, not just the parts that aren't working.

chapter three

How we become our kids' victims—and strategies to prevent parent burnout

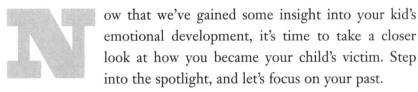ow that we've gained some insight into your kid's emotional development, it's time to take a closer look at how you became your child's victim. Step into the spotlight, and let's focus on your past.

How far back are we going? Way back. We're going to begin with the force that has the greatest influence on your parenting: the way you were parented. Your childhood holds the key to why you let your kid bully you.

Parenting isn't one-size-fits-all. It's a deeply rooted, personal experience. Parenting advice that doesn't consider your unique identity, history, or family culture is bound to fall short. Like a badly dubbed movie, one "parenting script" won't fit into the mouths of all parents. As I learned with my own kids, neither a mastery of child psychology nor a thorough knowledge of parenting strategies will help until you understand the profound impact of your own history and how it influences your parenting choices.

I'm not going to give you parenting advice that compromises your individuality. I won't force-feed you generic solutions. Lists of dos and don'ts are helpful reminders, but they rarely endure. Emotions run deep in parenting. In the end, the quickest and most effective way to produce change in your child isn't by manipulation, control, or domination. It begins with a good look in the mirror. It begins with you.

The Past Is Present

In parenting workshops, I ask moms and dads to close their eyes and imagine themselves at their children's age; to break away from the mundane, multitask-filled world of parenting and get in touch with the emotions they felt when they were kids.

Too often, parents forget how it felt back then. Sometimes, we hide behind our parenting authority as though we're all-knowing beings, doling out rewards and punishments. Or worst, we launch into heavy-handed lectures that elevate us while putting down our kids.

"When I was your age . . . blah, blah, blah."

What a bore!

As one teenager commented about his parents' badgering, "What's with adults? The minute they become parents, they forget what it's like to be a kid."

He was right! We forget what childhood feels like after we become parents. The less we identify with our kids and relate to their experience, the more conflict we're apt to have with them. Connecting with the feelings and experiences of our childhood brings us closer to our children and makes us more humanistic parents.

Let's get back to the parenting exercise. I want you to remember what it felt like to be parented. Revisiting your past will help you become more attuned to your kid. You'll begin to understand and appreciate her emotional state—her insecurities, fears, and anxieties. When you're better attuned, you'll be less inclined to judge, criticize, or blame. The more you identify with your kid's experience—and the more she feels understood by you—the less likely she'll be to engage in bullying behaviors.

So go ahead, think of yourself at your child's age. Take your time. Go for details.

> ➤ What are you wearing? Do you have a favorite jacket or shirt?

> ➤ How do you keep your hair? What length is it?

> ➤ What does your bedroom look like? How did you decorate it?

Now start writing. If you're not writing, start reflecting. Let your memories and associations flow unabated. Follow each image as it comes up. Take your time.

> ➤ What did you enjoy doing?

> ➤ What were you most insecure about?

> ➤ What social fears haunted you?

Not let's consider your parents.

Below is a list of questions. Explore them slowly—one at a time, or breeze through them all at once. Whatever suits you. The important thing is to record whatever springs to mind for each question. Go with the first memory. Be honest. Keep it simple. Trust that each memory holds another piece of your bullied-parent puzzle.

> ➤ What is your earliest memory of your parents?

> ➤ How old were you? Where were you living?

> ➤ What feelings accompany the memory?

Keep going. Be specific. Follow the memories as far as you can. If you have more than one memory, that's great. Flesh them out. We're searching for the unseen forces that shape your parenting. These memories hold the key.

NIGEL'S REALIZATION

While journaling, Nigel recalled that when he was a teenager, his father became very critical, constantly complaining and finding fault with Nigel's friends, his schoolwork, and his clothes. Nigel felt like he could never please his father and, in time, he gave up trying. Sadly, the two became alienated from each other and estranged as adults.

When Nigel reflected on his relationship with his son, he realized that he, too, had grown critical. He criticized the way that his son dressed and how he wore his hair. This was a prime trigger for his son's bullying behaviors. It horrified Nigel to think that he was repeating the negative pattern. After all, Nigel, who grew to hate his father, certainly didn't want his own kid to hate him.

Nigel knew that changing his own behavior was the key to rebuilding their relationship and disrupting the bullying dynamic between them. By evoking the emotional experience of his teen years, and recalling his feelings toward his father, Nigel was able to make a conscious break with negative patterns and move his relationship with his son in a new direction. Nigel's memories of his own teen years held the key to a deeper understanding of his son's behavior—and empathy changed his criticism to compassion.

Intellectual understanding without emotional identification brings limited results. If your kid is bullying you, there's a reason. As you journal about your own experience at your kid's age, you develop a

stronger identification with her and come to know the internal conflicts that are causing her to bully. Armed with greater empathy, you
are empowered to make better choices.

Are you ready to go on? Okay, let's digger deeper now.

The Light and Dark Sides of Your Parenting

In this next exercise, we'll explore the light and dark qualities of your
parents' behavior—their choices, tendencies, and habits. With a
watchful eye, we'll uncover how they affect you and impact your parenting today. Each memory will contain clues as to why you allow
your child to bully you.

If you had two parents, start by picking one, then repeat the exercise with the other parent.

Remember, parenting isn't always limited to actual parents. Feel
free to substitute any adult who played a parenting role in your life.
It could be an aunt or uncle, cousin, grandparent—anyone who cared
for you or had a big impact on you as a child.

Okay. Let's start with the lighter side.

> ➤ When were your parents most happy?

> ➤ What were their best qualities?

> ➤ When did you enjoy each parent the most?

Recall your memories in as much detail as you can. Now let's consider your parents' darker side:

> ➤ What were your parents' dark qualities?

> ➤ When was their mood the worst?

> ➤ What memory accompanies these feelings?

I've never met a parent who at some point didn't catch herself
repeating her parents' pet phrases. Everyone internalizes their parents'

good and bad qualities. It's a natural process, and becoming a parent awakens such memories from their slumber.

Let's consider the light and dark qualities you inherited from your parents and how they influence your parenting choices today.

> ➤ What light qualities did you inherit from your parents?

> ➤ What dark qualities did you inherit?

> ➤ Which qualities do you want to keep, and which do you want to jettison?

I'm always amazed when parents can vividly recall their own parents' words, moods, and deeds. It's a powerful reminder of how our childhood experiences affect our lives. During these exercises, many parents discover details that they had long forgotten. Some break down in tears, others recall good times that they had forgotten. Slowly, over time, they begin to see the massive influence that their parents' behavior has on their own parenting.

Here's a sample of a father's discoveries:

The Light Qualities
"My dad had a great sense of humor. When he was in a playful mood, he was so much fun. I have many happy memories of him chasing me around the house, playing tag and hide-and-go-seek. Sometimes we laughed so hard, my mother would worry about the neighbors. These are my most precious memories of him. He was so free and easy to be with when he was in a good mood."

The Dark Qualities
"My dad had a terrible temper, especially when he drank too much. He could be mean and sadistic, a real bully. He said things to me that I've never forgotten; his critical voice still lives in my head. Sometime I say things to my kids that he said to me. I hate myself when that happens. It scares me to death

that I could hurt my kids in the way my dad hurt me when he was in a dark mood."

Our parents' voices, positive and negative, take up residence in our minds and become a vital part of our identity, constantly influencing and advising us. Their attitudes, praise, criticisms, and complaints are alive in us.

Breaking negative patterns from your childhood requires making a conscious choice. It will take consistent effort to move your parenting in a brand new direction. Deep changes in intergenerational family patterns do not come easily, nor do they come of their own accord.

I've had hundreds of sessions with bullied parents suffering from all kinds of personal problems, from depression and anxiety to relationship issues and professional insecurities. What is the number one topic that comes up? Their relationship with their parents. In session after session, they revisit the childhood memories of their parents—sometimes for years.

Parents are towering figures in our unconscious minds. They loom over us, even more so when we become parents. The power of these early experiences cannot be overstated, particularly when it comes to the way they influence how you interact with your child.

Will you repeat your parents' choices, spend your lifetime opposing them, or forge a new path?

Step into the Spotlight
In this final exercise, be as honest as possible. Don't hold back. Challenge yourself to complete the following sentences:

> ➤ My light qualities as a parent are . . . .

> ➤ My dark qualities as a parent are . . .

> ➤ The parenting choices I always regret are . . .

> ➤ The personal behaviors I want to change the most are . . .

Look for patterns and themes. Can you see your own history in the parenting choices you make? Now identify the parts of your parents that you want to keep and the parts you want to lose.

COOKING UP A HEALTHIER RELATIONSHIP

Liana grew nostalgic while journaling about her mother's light qualities. She recalled how much she loved cooking with her mom: "My mother was so much fun in the kitchen," she wrote. "She had this gift. She seemed to make up recipes on the spot. We went on culinary adventures together, inventing dishes as we went along. Cooking with her was so much fun! Some of my best childhood memories are in her kitchen."

When Liana reflected on her relationship with her own daughter, Zoe, she realized that there wasn't a single activity that they enjoyed together. She lamented that they never even cooked one meal together. In fact, they had fallen into the habit of ordering fast food. How sad to think that Zoe's memory of Liana would be her calling out for home delivery!

After journaling about these memories and sharing them with her husband, Liana went out and bought two new aprons, one for her and one for Zoe. That night, she told Zoe that they would be cooking together two days a week—and what's more, Zoe would also be in charge of planning an entire family meal once a week.

Of course, Zoe was incredulous. "Are you serious?" she asked her mom. "Cooking is so boring. It's so much easier to order in."

However, in the weeks that followed, as Zoe learned her way around the kitchen, she began to love it. Soon, she was even preparing meals for her friends. Liana was delighted. "I thought my love of cooking died when my mother died," she said. "I was wrong. The day Zoe started inventing dishes and calling me into the kitchen yelling, 'Hey, Mom, come taste this!' I had tears in my eyes. It was like having a bit of my mom back with us."

The Parents Most Likely to Be Bullied

Over the years, as I listened to bullied parents' stories, I began to recognize many common experiences. Though bullied parents come from difficult cultures and communities, I've identified the three most common scenarios that contribute to parents allowing their kids to bully them.

Of course, these are broad categories; parents are much more complex than the snapshot histories presented here. Yet, you may find them to be generally applicable—and food for thought.

The parents most likely to be bullied by their kids are:

➤ Parents who were bullied by their own parents

➤ Parents who had absent or neglectful parents

➤ Parents who had narcissistic parents

Let's consider each scenario, and see if they ring true for you.

Bullied by Their Own Parents

Many parents who are bullied by their children were themselves bullied by their own parents. The culture of bullying endures from generation to generation, only the roles change.

In defiance of their history, parents who were bullied by their parents may overcompensate with their own children. For example, adults who grew up in homes with overly strict parents tend to be too liberal and permissive with their kids. In a strange way, they set out to undo their history with their own kids by giving them the freedom that they were denied. These parents often made a vow in their youth: "When I grow up, I'm never going to treat my kids the way I was treated." Determined that their kids will not suffer the way they did, they parent in opposition to their parent's choices. This backlash against authoritarian parenting of the past is often at the heart of the bullied parenting dilemma that we find ourselves in today. For example:

> ➤ If your parents were dominating, you might overcompensate by being too accommodating and permissive.

> ➤ If your parents were critical, you might strive to be more of a friend than a parent to your child.

> ➤ If your parents were inattentive, you might smother your kid with attention and become overly involved in his life.

Bullied parents' hearts are in the right place. After all, they want their kids to have a better childhood than they did. Yet, their overreaching efforts to undo the pain of their own history will prevent them from providing the leadership their kids need for healthy social and emotional development.

Such parents tend to avoid any parenting decisions that may anger their child. In fact, they begin to fear their kid, just as they feared their parents. As the trauma of their own childhood is awakened, they stop thinking like adults and start thinking like children.

MEET BRADLEY THE BULLY

Hazel described her eleven-year-old son, Bradley, as a tyrannical bully. He yelled at her, called her names, and mocked her. A single mother with no support, she felt overwhelmed by Bradley's aggressive behavior. One difficult night, he was so verbally abusive that Hazel actually called the police.

The police believed they were going to the scene of domestic violence. When they arrived and Hazel explained that her son was abusing her, they asked to speak with him. Then, when little Bradley came out of his bedroom in his pajamas, the police enjoyed a hearty laugh.

Bradley was threatening her? This tiny child? Was she serious?

If we consider Hazel's upbringing, it's clear why she was afraid: Bradley's verbal abuse had awakened the trauma of her parents abusing her. As a child, no one had come to Hazel's aid. Subsequently, when she began to relive the feelings of fear and powerlessness from her childhood, she did what she couldn't do as a child: she called for help. To Hazel, it made perfect sense.

As you can see, parents who were bullied by their parents have to struggle through a mess of personal anxieties and emotional traumas that are awakened when they become parents. For Hazel to make new parenting choices, she had to understand how her parents' abuse impacts her parenting today.

Absent or Neglectful Parents

Adults who grew up with absent or neglectful parents have a particularly difficult time being parents because they had no parental model to internalize. Even if they had a mother or father, they felt parentless.

Unsurprisingly, when they become parents, they haven't a clue what to do. With no parenting model to follow or oppose, they feel lost and overwhelmed in their new role.

Desperate, they defer decisions and avoid unpopular parenting choices. They may even shift the burden of parenting onto the shoulders of their own kids, letting them make parenting decisions for themselves.

Though kids jump at the chance to seize leadership from their parents, they are totally unprepared to manage themselves. They can't structure their day, set their own schedule, or plan for their future. Without the guiding hand of a confident parent, it's only a matter of time before they stumble and become bullies.

No kid wants to parent himself.

MEET MAX AND HIS MISSING PARENT

Max put it succinctly: "How can I know how to be a dad—when I never had a dad?"

Raised by his mother and her sisters, Max never knew what it was like to have a father. Now as a dad raising two girls, he became flustered by the simplest of parenting decisions. He feared making the wrong choice or hurting his kids, so whenever possible he deferred to his wife. Eventually, his kids demanded answers from him. After all, he was their father.

Max's situation went from bad to worse when his tween daughter, Tonya, began to bully him. Max had no clue how to respond. "I learned about fatherhood from sitcoms," he said. "But those dads had scripts—I didn't. And none of them had kids who spoke to him like Tonya spoke to me."

After many therapy sessions, lots of journaling, and learning to apply the tools in this book, Max overcame his fears and provided the leadership Tonya needed.

Max's breakthrough moment? He stopped letting his past define him. "I got tired of my story and decided to write a new one," he said. "I decided to be the dad that I wanted to have when I was a kid."

Max's new confidence enabled him to put a stop to Tonya's bullying and heal his past.

A Narcissistic Parent

Narcissistic parents are often hard to spot. They attend school events and parent/teacher conferences. They throw birthday parties. From a distance, they seem like ideal parents. So why are they bullied by their children?

Take a closer look and you'll see the problem hiding in plain sight. They are terrible listeners and conversation monopolizers. Incessantly self-referential, rather than respecting and promoting their kids' individuality, they try to make them mini-versions of themselves.

For children, nothing is more enraging than not being recognized by your own parent.

Kids often bully in an effort to break through a parent's self-absorption. But narcissistic parents are too wrapped up in themselves to identify with their kids, steering conversations back to themselves, fixating on their own childhoods, telling endless stories about the past or forcing their kids to endure tiresome yarns about their own achievements.

The problem here is that narcissistic parents don't live in the moment. This creates a profound sense of emotional deprivation in their children. And it fuels bullying. Every child has three basic emotional needs: to be listened to, to be recognized, and to be validated by their parents. Self-absorption prevents narcissistic parents from meeting any of these needs.

When adolescence hits, and kids begin to claim their own separate ideas and identities, narcissistic parents are likely to view it as a betrayal. Conflicts escalate.

Sadly, most relationships between a narcissistic parent and a bullying kid end in estrangement. Unless the parent changes his ways, the relationship is doomed.

MEET KIT: A BULLY'S ANGUISH

No kid wants to bully his parents. For one thing, it has a devastating effect on self-esteem. The more a kid bullies, the worse he feels about himself. Deep down, he wants his parents to take a stand. Such was the case with Kit.

Kit was quiet in high school. He was mild-mannered and soft-spoken. But at home he was a vicious bully to his mother.

Why did Kit act like two different children?

At one meeting I had with Kit and his mom, she was, as usual, describing details about her own life. In fact, she spoke obsessively about herself. Each time a story wound down and I thought she had finished, she launched into another story.

Kit, sitting beside her on the couch, tried to interrupt her a number of times with a question or an elaboration. She simply talked over him: *"Let me finish."*

But there was no end to her talking. It was a wonder that she had time to breathe.

The entire time Kit was held hostage. Whenever he spoke, she ignored him, or spoke over him. "Let me finish," she said.

After several attempts, Kit's face grew taut; red blotches appeared on his neck. The more she spoke, the redder he became. Then suddenly, before my eyes, Kit hauled off and punched his mother, knocking her onto her side. I had never before seen such an act of violence in my office.

I was enraged. "You are never going to hit your mother again!" I demanded. Do you understand? No matter how angry you feel, you are not allowed to hit her."

Kit and I had a very friendly relationship. He had never seen me angry, and the force of my voice shocked him. Before he could respond, his mother jumped in with an apology. "He didn't mean it," she said, "He can't control himself."

Kit began to weep. He pressed his fists to his eyes and lowered his head in shame. Hot tears rolled down his cheeks. His mother reached out and touched his arm. "It's okay, honey. This is why you need help."

Kit hid his face as his mother embarked on another long story about herself. It was the last thing he needed. She was telling Kit that he, not her parenting, was defective.

Are You a Burned Out Parent?

Before we go any further, I'd like to say a word or two about why so many bullied parents suffer from parent burnout.

This book is meant to challenge you, to start a revolution in your parenting and empower you. Its ultimate goal is to end bullying in your household. But before we can do that, I'm going to need you to take better care of yourself. Standing up to your kid's bullying will require more energy and stamina, both of which are impossible to muster when you're burned out.

Most bullied parents don't even realize that they're suffering from parent burnout. Ask these parents when was the last time they took a break from parenting, and they stare at you stupefied:

"You're allowed to take a break?"

Kids who bully are gifted crisis creators. They are demanding, pushy, and aggressive—and they only become more so with age. Unfortunately, the more time you spend accommodating them, the less time you spend taking caring for yourself, and the more likely your kid will bully you.

Living in a state of chronic self-neglect negatively impacts every area of your life—your relationships, career, family, and friendships—and empowers your kid's abuse. When you're just too fatigued to put a stop to the bullying, you're inadvertently supporting it.

If you don't respect your own needs, your kid won't, either. You're the one who sets the tone for the relationship.

When you're tired all the time, it's easy to slip into a victim role. Children with burned-out parents always feel burdened by their parent's unhappiness. When a parent goes around lamenting about his life, grumbling about all the inconveniences of parenting, it puts his kid on the defensive. He feels like he's getting blamed for his parent's unhappiness.

You may blame others for your feelings of neglect, but only you can remedy it.

Burned-out parents neglect their needs and end up depleted emotionally, intellectually, and creatively. Spend some time with them and you will actually begin to feel their weariness. They zone out in the middle of conversations, stare in a hypnotic trance, or go through the same routines mindlessly. Is it any wonder that they don't have the energy to stand up to their kid's bullying?

As I said earlier, most burned-out parents don't even know that they're burned out. So, let's take an inventory of your life. If you answer yes to four or more of the following questions, chances are, burnout is coming your way:

PARENT'S BURNOUT QUIZ

❏ Are you growing humorless?

❏ Has romance gone out of your relationship?

❏ Have you stopped hanging out with friends?

❏ Do you feel dog-tired all the time?

❏ Do you fret about spending money on a babysitter?

❏ Do you feel guilty when you treat yourself to something special?

❏ Do you have trouble remembering when you had a day off from parenting?

❏ Does every conversation eventually come back to the subject of your kids?

❏ Have you stopped exercising or going to the gym?

❏ Has complaining become a way of life?

How to Cure Parent Burnout

It will be impossible to transform your relationship with your kid unless you transform your relationship with yourself. Putting a stop to bullying starts with valuing yourself more than you do now.

To get your life back on track, you don't need to spend a fortune on therapy, European vacations, or gym memberships. In the previous chapter, I gave you a five-point checklist for your kid. Now here's a four-point checklist for you.

PARENT'S BURNOUT PREVENTION CHECKLIST

❑ *Say hello to "me time."*

❑ *Get moving.*

❑ *Get creative.*

❑ *Get out of town.*

1. Say Hello to "Me Time"

➤ Does a quiet hotel room sound like heaven?

➤ How about a drive alone?

➤ Are you excited by the thought of someone else serving you?

When you have a bullying kid, putting time aside for yourself is surprisingly difficult, especially when you've fallen into the habit of self-neglect.

Parenting is not the world's longest act of self-sacrifice, nor should it be. Burned-out parents teach their children that life is one endless grind of joyless responsibilities. And the heaviness of burnout weighs their children down.

No kid respects burned-out parents, which is why he feels free to bully them.

Kids want their parents to have passions. They want to be proud of them. After all, if their parents are happy and successful in life, it means that they too can be happy and successful. Being that kind of role model is a must for parents.

If you're a member of the Burned-Out Parent Club, severing your membership begins with putting time aside for yourself. Maybe spend some time journaling, rereading a favorite book, or doing an activity that you enjoy—something that will quiet your mind and bring you some peace.

You won't find time for yourself until you make time for yourself. Better self-care is the best step you can take to improve your relationship with your child and stop the bullying in your household.

2. Get Moving

> ➤ Do you feel drained all the time?

> ➤ Do you have a love affair with the snooze button on your alarm clock?

> ➤ Are your midday naps becoming epic?

Burned-out parents complain of a lack of energy or motivation. When I recommend exercising or working out, I get blank stares or protests.

"I'm already so exhausted. You want me to add exercise to my schedule?"

MEET ALICE: FIGHTING FOR HER LIFE

Alice had every reason to feel discouraged. When her husband ran off with his high school crush (whom he'd found online), he left her alone to raise their two teen daughters, Christina and Stacy. Alice was in a state of shock. Eventually, she fell into a dark depression. Unfortunately, she soothed her hurt by binge eating.

Six months and fifty pounds later, Alice found herself in the worst physical shape of her life. What's more, she was forgetting appointments and frequently arriving late to work.

She spent her weekends in bed watching television and eating junk food.

Christina and Stacy hated to see their mother so defeated. To them, she had given up on herself. Initially, they felt bad for her. But eventually, they resented her. They bullied her, mocking her weight and poking fun at her tight-fitting clothes and her discomfort in heels.

"Why stop at three donuts? Have the whole box."

"Maybe you can be a plus-size model."

"No wonder dad left you."

Deep down, Alice wondered if they were right. She knew that she had to do something, but she hated working out. Every time she made an appointment with a trainer, she got as far as the front door of the gym before turning around, going home, and getting back in bed.

After a particularly dreadful medical checkup and a scolding from her doctor, Alice called a friend and set a weekly jogging date.

The first run was pure hell. As her friend chatted away, Alice gasped for air and took many breaks. When it was finally over, she felt humiliated.

However, she pressed on. Running once a week, then twice and three times. Each run became a little easier. Then something caught Alice's eye.

Alice and her friend's jogging route took them by a boxing gym. In the window, boxers danced around, hitting bags, jumping rope, sparing. Boy, did that look like fun! Alice wondered if they had boxing lessons for women. So she phoned the gym to find out.

They did.

Alice's hands shook on the steering wheel as she drove to her first lesson. "I don't think I have the courage to go through with this," she thought to herself. "I should turn the car around and go home. What will people think of me?"

Alice wrestled with her thoughts right up until she parked her car outside the gym. She took a deep breath. A new way of thinking was taking root in her. She was tired of evading challenges and caring so much what others thought.

Alice was tired of her old story.

From the moment Alice threw her first punch, she was hooked. She loved everything about boxing: wrapping her hands, tying on the gloves. She even liked the smell of the place. And hitting those bags—man, did that feel good!

Alice came home from boxing lessons drenched in sweat. Practicing her routine in the bathroom mirror, she bragged to Christina and Stacy that her trainer said she was a natural.

Of course, Alice's daughters were skeptical. "A forty-year-old woman, boxing? Really, Mom?"

Alice responded with a shrug. It felt so good that she didn't care what anyone thought. After a few weeks, she told her trainer she wanted to try a few rounds in the ring with a real opponent. When Christina and Stacy asked if they could come and watch, Alice was thrilled but responded offhandedly. "Sure. Why not?"

In a matter of weeks, Alice became a sensation. Her daughters bragged about her and took their friends to see her matches. Alice was suddenly cool. She felt better than she had in years. She also had an important revelation: She realized how unhappy she'd been in her marriage. For years, she'd lived in a fog.

Alice's husband had always been an oppressive force in her life. He was critical and negative, always putting her down. No wonder her daughters bullied her. They were following their father's lead!

But when Alice started taking better care of herself, everything changed.

In no time, Christina and Stacy lost interest in bullying their mom. On rare occasions, when they did give her a hard time, Alice responded: "You want to go a few rounds in the ring and settle this?"

Of course they didn't. More important, they didn't need to.

Boxing not only cured Alice's parent burnout, it was the knockout punch that ended her daughters' bullying once and for all.

Parents need tension outlets just like their kids. Walk, run, swim, bike, tap dance—whatever tickles your fancy. Remember, a cardio workout, thirty minutes, three times a week can dramatically reduce symptoms of depression and anxiety. You'll feel better. You'll have more energy and less appetite. If you have trouble committing to a weekly workout, sign up for a class, get a trainer, find a gym buddy, or take a lesson from Alice and go for a jog!

3. Get Creative

> ➤ Is buying your kid a new lunchbox your idea of being creative?

> ➤ Do you consider doodling on your phone bill an artistic activity?

> ➤ When your kids tell you to "get a life," do you wonder if they're right?

Let's face it, parenting is often dull, repetitive work: cooking meals, buying clothes, helping with homework, driving your kids to soccer games or band practice, picking them up after school or from the mall. If you're lulled into feeling like a taxi service or a maid, if you respond to each new day with a weary shrug, it's time to think about putting more creative energy into your own life.

Creativity is a natural stress reliever. It soothes angst, awakens your muse, and brings new dynamism into your day. It will lift your spirits and give you a much-needed break from the mundane world of day-to-day parenting. You'll also have more energy to tame that nerve-racking bully in your home.

You'll be amazed how much better you will feel and how much more energy you'll have when you awaken your creative self.

The Burned-Out Parent Breakfast Club My first job after grad school was coordinating a counseling program at a struggling elementary school in Brooklyn. Each morning, I'd watch a parade of blurry-eyed burned-out parents drop their kids off and stumble back onto the street. Since my program was charged with helping students succeed, I decided the best place to start would be to help their parents.

When letters, phone calls, and mailings to students' homes yielded zero replies, I decided to try a different tactic: I posted signs all over the school.

FREE BREAKFAST FOR PARENTS

As parents dropped their kids off, I lured them to my office with the smell of fresh coffee and baked goods. (I'd even set up a small fan beside the coffee machine to push the smell into the halls.)

Slowly, one by one, they stumbled into my office—breakfast zombies in search of a freebie.

Within a few hours, I had a dozen parents sign up for my first parenting group.

Rather than lecture them on child rearing or psychology, I decided a little creativity would be far more fun.

In the first workshop, I gave each parent a bucket of art supplies. They had poster board and construction paper at their disposal. I encouraged them to create anything they wanted. Whatever tickled their fancies.

The parents poked at the supplies, and peered at me out of the corners of their eyes. Being creative was an everyday event for kids. But for burned-out parents, it was completely foreign. They had no idea what to do.

Gradually, as parents sipped coffee and downed donuts, they sheepishly began to use the art supplies. They began to sketch, paint, and draw. And once they started, they couldn't stop. Some worked quietly, in deep meditation. Others chatted and laughed playfully.

The workshop was scheduled for ninety minutes, but nearly everyone stayed an hour or two longer and continued working.

"Why are they taking so long?" I wondered.

Then it dawned on me. These parents are starved for creativity! Their imaginations are aching for a workout. Since becoming parents, they've had no creative time for themselves. The simple act of sitting alone and being creative was so invigorating that they could barely contain themselves. Creativity was an exciting and invigorating journey back to their pre-parent selves.

In the weeks that followed, kids dropped by my office to see what their parents had made. That was when I learned another important lesson: The kids loved to see their parents being creative.

"My mom did that? Awesome."

"My dad's picture is so cool."

"I didn't know my mom could draw."

The kids were thrilled to discover a side of their parents that they didn't know.

After the workshop, many parents brought their art project home and kept working on it. They continued to be creative for one simple reason: It felt good.

When parents begin to feel better about their own selves, they begin to be better parents. Rediscovering their creative side not only helped cure their burnout but also infused positive energy into their relationship with their kids.

So it's time to get out your old paint set, camera, sewing kit, or toolbox. Build something in your garage, plant something in your garden. These tasks are as important to parenting as feeding and providing for your family.

What would you like to create?

4. Get Out of Town

> ➤ Do you sleepwalk through your daily routines?

> ➤ Is visiting the fruit section of your grocery store your idea of an exotic vacation?

> ➤ Do travel magazines look like fantasy novels?

Bullied parents don't spend enough time in the parent-free world beyond their front door. Worse, the more they sacrifice for their kids, the more their kids take them for granted.

When you stop traveling, visiting friends, or going out for a bit of fun, your parenting is headed toward burnout. You need a break from your kids just as much as they need a break from you.

Finding alone time with your spouse or making space for friends or new activities nourishes the burned-out soul. It's a great way to rejuvenate your life so you can stand up to your kid's bullying.

That means making a plan for quality nonparenting time. So, pick up the phone, call an old friend, reconnect with acquaintances—whenever it takes to break free of isolation. Get out of your house, socialize, go to a comedy club, see a concert, visit an art gallery, take a hike. Yes, get out of town! Any effort you make to try something new will bring fresh energy into your parenting.

MEET ELENA AND JOHN

When Elena and John walked into my office, I could feel their exhaustion. Before children, they were full of hopes and dreams. By the time their third son was born, every day was a struggle with despair.

John was losing his temper more and sounding an awful lot like his father. Elena struggled mightily with feelings of depression and hopelessness. In response to their low state of life, their kids began to bully them with back talk and full-throated public meltdowns.

Elena and John felt embarrassed by their children's behavior, but were too tired to do anything about it.

When I suggested time off from parenting, they scoffed. They didn't have the budget to travel or pay a babysitter for more than an hour or two. They shot down my suggestions without consideration or reflection. Like many burned-out parents, their outlook was gloomy.

So I came up with a plan: Since the boys were in school all day, could John arrange his work schedule to take a morning or two off? Maybe a long lunch?

"Well . . . it's possible. But is that really a vacation?"

It wasn't a vacation, but it was a start.

Elena and John began by having a quiet breakfast together. In the process, they discovered something that they had forgotten: They enjoyed each other's company. It was like they were dating again.

They tried a morning yoga class. Sometimes they went to an art gallery or played tennis after dropping their kids off at school. Afterward, John sometimes jogged to work and Elena found the energy to start working on her long-abandoned novel again.

When Elena and John made more time for fun and creativity in their life, it rejuvenated their marriage and their parenting. Even their sex life improved. Most important, they had the energy to put an end to their boys' bullying and enforce new structure, limits, and boundaries around their home.

It's impossible to stop your kid's bullying when you are depleted and drained. Curing your parent burnout goes hand-in-hand with curing bullying. Good self-care is good child-care. It breathes new energy into your life and the stamina to tackle your kid's bullying.

In the next chapter, we're going to identify your child's bullying style and show you immediate steps that you can take to resolve it.

chapter four

Understanding your kid's bullying behavior style

kay, let's do a quick recap.

In Chapter 1, we explored the bully two-step, and came to understand how you and your kid are partners in this ungainly dance. In Chapter 2, we did a quick primer on child development and considered the immediate steps and long-term interventions you can take to address bullying. In Chapter 3, we looked at the light and dark sides of your parenting and picked up some parent burnout prevention strategies.

In this chapter, we'll look at the different bullying styles kids use. While all children have unique personalities and temperaments, those who bully their parents have many traits in common. To work as simply as possible, I've sorted them into three distinct bullying styles: the *defiant bully*, the *anxious bully*, and the *manipulative bully*.

These three bullying styles are presented in a broad fashion. After all, children's personalities are too complex to fit into tidy little categories. The bullying styles presented here are designed to offer you a lens through which to view your child's behavior. With a clearer understanding of your kid's bullying style, you will gain a deeper understanding of her inner life and be better prepared to steer your relationship in a new direction.

A single bullying style may fit your kid perfectly, or she may meet the criteria for more than one. As you mull over the questions presented at the outset of each section, ask yourself which style best captures your child.

Throughout this process, keep in mind that beneath the tough exterior of every bully is a scared child with an unstable core, constantly wrestling with insecurities and worries. Bullying is an expression of such internal unrest. By understanding what makes your bully tick, you will gain insight into the nature of her fears and better understand the forces that fuel her bullying.

The Defiant Bully

Let's begin with the most brassy and cantankerous type of them all: the defiant bully.

Kids with a Defiant Bullying Style

> Does your kid back you into a corner with demands and threats?

> Are you afraid of your kid's anger?

> Do you dread your kid's outbursts?

> Is your kid always opposing you?

> Does your kid blackmail you?

> Do you fear saying no and inciting your kid's wrath?

> Have you felt terrorized by your kid?

> Does your kid torment you until you give into his demands?

> Does your kid blame you for her problems?

> Do you feel controlled by your kid?

The most challenging of the bullying personality types, these in-your-face kids are exceedingly confrontational and oppositional. If you say, "Go right," they go left. If you say, "Sit still," they run.

Impulsive, impatient, and reckless, defiant bullies want to live on their own terms. They reject every attempt their parents make to manage their behavior. If you're a single parent, defiant kids can be particularly aggressive. With only one parent to focus on, you're more likely to get a double-dose of defiance!

Self-righteous and puffed up with false confidence, defiant kids delight in debate and are determined to win every argument. Being "right" takes priority over being respectful or getting along. When you try to stand up to their bullying, they turn obsessive and harass you until you give in. Determined to get their way, they'll stop at nothing to defeat you.

The Good and Bad News about Defiance

Defiance is not necessarily a problematic trait. Many artists, inventors, designers, and original thinkers have a healthy defiant streak in them. They pioneer new ways of thinking because they oppose conventions. They use their defiance as a creative force for inspiration and vision.

In other words, when defiance is fused with ambition and channeled into creativity, it is progressive. Defiant kids have a lot of unbridled and unfocused energy. The challenge is to help them channel it into a positive outlet.

Every well-adjusted kid has a healthy dose of defiance. If children are too cooperative or accommodating, they lack definition and leave no lasting imprint on others. You don't want your kid to agree with you all the time. You want her to have her own opinions and views.

Here's the bad news about defiance: It's going to take a lot of effort to help a kid with a defiant bullying style see any relationship as a two-way street. The longer the pattern has been in place, the more difficult it is to reverse. It takes energy and commitment to help a defiant kid break old habits and foster new ones.

What Drives the Defiant Kid?

Underneath the bravado of defiance is a kid who, for some reason, feels unrecognized and undervalued. She lives with a fear of being forgotten or left out. No matter how much attention she gets, positive or negative, it's rarely enough.

You'd never how vulnerable defiant kids feel because they conceal their insecurities so well. For example, they may look disheveled, but a lot of thought has gone into looking just the ideal amount of disheveled. In public, they might not seem to care, but in private they fret about their image, obsessing about their appearance, clothes, and hairstyle.

Ultimately, defiance is a form of dependency. Here's why: In order to feel whole, defiant kids must have something to *defy*. Pushing against someone or something gives them a false sense of strength. For example, imagine a kid leaning against a wall. He may appear secure but what happens when you take the wall away? He falls down. Defiance works in the same way. Without someone or something to defy, defiant kids can't keep their stance.

What do defiant kids gain from their defiance? Defiance forms a protective barrier against interpersonal insecurities, providing a temporary identity for kids who feel uncertain about their individuality. Kids with a defiant bullying style are easily misinterpreted: Their defiance creates the illusion that they are strong and secure, when actually it's just the opposite. Spend enough time with defiant kids and you'll sense their insecurities just below the surface.

CHARLIE'S NO ANGEL

I recall Charlie, a tattooed, wild-haired young man about twenty years old. He contacted me for a consultation and demanded an appointment as soon as possible. While speaking with him on the telephone, I could tell I was dealing with a defiant bully. No matter what their age, defiant bullies all sound like bossy children.

Charlie, who told me he slept during the day, declined every appointment time I offered and demanded I stay late to see him. He'd dropped out of high school (twice) and recently was suspended from college (again) for reasons he refused to explain. So, why the appointment? He needed a letter from a therapist stating that he was in therapy so he could return to class.

He arrived to the appointment late, breathless, and sweaty, with a bicycle slung over his shoulder. The doorman wouldn't let him in the building with the bike, so he snuck into the freight elevator and found his way to my office.

Once he entered, I was assaulted by his potent body odor—a smell I would later dub "Scent of Charlie."

Almost immediately, he began to complain. Everyone was out to get him—his school, his parents, even my doorman. He took no responsibility for his behavior, the hallmark of a defiant bully.

Sensing he would never return after receiving a letter from me, I told him I would consider writing the letter for him after he attended three sessions. I needed to get to know him better so I could represent him more accurately.

"Bull**it!" Charlie barked, and stormed out without paying me.

In retrospect, I was too accommodating to Charlie from the get-go. I adjusted my schedule to his needs too quickly, giving him the sense that he was in charge of my time. Kids with defiant bullying styles have a special talent for getting their way.

Charlie's bullying for an appointment had caught me off guard, and I'd surrendered to his will without thought. The problem is, if you accommodate defiant bullies too quickly, they lose respect for you. Charlie walked out because I failed to hold my own in the face of his bullying.

Years later, Charlie returned. This time I didn't bend. We set the appointment based on my schedule. Surprisingly, he didn't put up a fight.

Charlie, still sweaty and tattooed, looked in deep despair. He arrived on time (Scent of Charlie in tow) and collapsed on my couch looking defeated. When I asked why he'd returned, he sighed. "I screwed up my life."

"What do you mean?" I asked.

He closed his eyes; this was going to be painful to say. "I never listened to my parents or my teachers. I fought against people like you who wanted to help me. Now I have nothing."

He went on to explain that he had to sell his bike to pay off his weed dealer and other debts.

As he spoke, I felt as if I was sitting with a person who, by his own accord, was bankrupt in every sense of the word. His unrestrained defiance had left him with nothing to show for himself—not a single accomplishment to take pride in, not one healthy relationship.

Let's get under the skin of a defiant bully and learn what makes her tick.

PARENTING DILEMMA: MEET SARA

Age: 13 and a half
Bullying Style: Defiant
Favorite Bullying Tactics: Tantrums, threats, and meltdowns
Bullying Moment:

"I hate you! It's all your fault!"

When Sara found out that she didn't get into the middle school she wanted, it was a toxic dose of heartbreak and public humiliation. Every day, as friends brashly waved their acceptance letters in the air like victory flags, Sara hid in the bathroom, sobbing.

In truth, Sara had put little effort into her middle school application. She'd expected to be automatically accepted. Now she was bitter with defeat. Annoying "shoulds" tortured her at night:

I should have worked harder on my application.

I should have studied more for prep tests.

I should have rehearsed for my interviews.

These thoughts haunted Sara. To free herself from the burden of responsibility, she did what defiant bullies often do—she blamed her parents.

From the moment the middle school placement letter arrived in June, and throughout the endless summer, Sara bullied her parents unmercifully. It was their failure, not hers. They hadn't helped her enough, they didn't care for her enough, and they didn't love her enough.

Sara's parents, Marcus and Lisa, felt overwhelmed with guilt and accepted much of the blame. (We'll get to know guilty parents in Chapter 5.) Troubling "shoulds" kept Marcus and List up at night, too:

We should have made her work harder on her application.

We should have demanded that she prepare more.

We should have been more involved in the application process.

While Sara and her parents were "should having" all over themselves, their home was gloomy, at best. With no tension outlets, Sara began binge-eating her way through the summer.

Finally, the first day of school arrived. As Sara angrily stomped her way toward the unfamiliar building, Lisa and Marcus watched from their car and held their breath.

Maybe it wouldn't be so bad?

Maybe Sara would surprise them?

Maybe she would like it?

Yeah, right.

➤ ➤ ➤

"I'm not going back tomorrow!" Sara screamed as she entered the house that afternoon after school. "You suck as parents! You're stupid! You ruined my life! I hate you both!"

Marcus and Lisa did their best to calm Sara, but their attempts only brought more abuse. She screamed, howled, threw books and shoes, and cursed at them.

Marcus and Lisa soon became battle weary; this was beyond anything they'd ever seen. "Should we's" kept them up at night:

➤ Should we arrange for home schooling?

➤ Should we look at boarding schools?

➤ Should we force her to go back to school?

To understand the true causes of Sara's suffering, let's take a deep look into her past.

Sara's History

Sara is going through a series of difficult transitions, from changing schools to losing friends, from enduring a long, isolated summer to experiencing stress-related weight gain, not to mention other upsetting events that she has chosen to hide from her parents. To get a fuller picture of the causes of her bullying, let's examine all aspects of her life.

Precocious Puberty

Puberty came unusually early for Sara and caused her much unease in school and in public. She developed breasts earlier than any of her friends; by fifth grade, boys ridiculed her in gym class; girls snickered in the lunchroom. To make matters worse, Sara refused to wear a bra (not a good decision).

Like many kids, Sara felt too humiliated to share this information with her parents. Kids in their early teens frequently hide their hardships from their parents out of fear of their parents' disappointment or judgment.

Struggling alone is always worse than struggling with the love and support of family. Sara's choices isolated her socially, and she withdrew even further.

Learning Differences

Sara has great difficulty organizing her notes, her handwriting is barely legible, and she has a history of reading difficulties. Doing homework with her parents often ends in tears or fights. So Marcus and Lisa arranged for a tutor to help Sara three times a week. Unfortunately, it's likely that Sara's learning difficulties are way beyond a tutor's capacity.

Kids with undiagnosed learning problems suffer low self-esteem due to their inability to keep up with their classmates or complete tests or assignments on time. The chronic tension that they experience in class also makes them moody and easily fatigued.

For Sara, who already had self-esteem issues, failing academically was yet another insult to her sense of well-being.

Sara's Secret Fears

Sara is convinced that her older brother, Edward, is her parent's favorite child. Everything appears to come so easily to Edward. Edward won a scholarship to college. Edward is popular. Edward does well in school. Marcus and Lisa even appear more at ease with him.

Every night in bed, Sara is tormented by negative self-talk:

I'm fat.

No one likes me.

I'm dumb.

Sara barely gets any sleep. Now, everything irritates her—the way her mother hums in the kitchen, the way her father chews his food, her brother's alarm clock (1980s rock).

As you can see, there's a whole lot going on with Sara. To make lasting gains, her parents need a multitiered approach. Let's start with steps they can take immediately to address her bullying.

Immediate Interventions

The first order of business is to help lower Sara's stress level and get her anger under control. Remember, beneath all her yelling and shouting is a deeply unhappy child.

Rather than try to force Sara back to school, punish her, or respond to her bullying in kind (all choices that will escalate conflicts and defiance), Marcus and Lisa would do better to give Sara a break: Let her miss a day of school and catch up on sleep.

Sending Sara to school exhausted and irritable will only make matters worse. At the same time, they should make it clear to Sara that they will consider other schooling options, but until then, she will have to continue to attend her current school.

This will set the stage for Sara to work collaboratively with her parents and demonstrate to her that her parents are listening and taking her seriously.

For kids in pain, listening is healing; feeling understood is a soothing balm for hurt. Sara may be thrashing about, bullying and threatening because she doesn't feel heard or understood by her parents. If Sara feels listened to and validated by her parents, she is less likely to bully them.

Next we want to introduce some self-soothing activities. For example, does Sara enjoy cooking with her mom or dad? Does she have any creative outlets or friends that she can turn to for support? Perhaps she and her father can spend a day together doing an activity that they enjoy.

When kids feel like they're facing insurmountable obstacles, it may help them to get a little distance. Harping on problems can increase stress and tension, and make difficulties worse. A day off from school would also give Sara the time and space she needs to lower the tension she feels and express the insecurities that she bottles up.

One last note: When approaching sensitive subjects with your defiant kid, one parent is often better than two. Kids often report feeling ganged up on or outnumbered when both parents approach them together. This increases defensiveness and tension. So, decide which parent is best for the job beforehand, clarify your goals, and remain united no matter what your kid throws at you.

These immediate steps are designed to lower the tension Sara feels inside and de-escalate the conflicts with her parents. Once she is more stable and rested, Marcus and Lisa should consider the following recommendations.

An Educational Evaluation Sara demonstrates many signs of nonverbal learning differences. That means she may function well verbally but has difficulty in nonverbal tasks, such as reading or writing. She struggles to complete assignments, tires more quickly, and suffers mood swings. She often hides her work, loses it, or forgets to hand it in to avoid the embarrassment of another low grade. These are all symptoms of undiagnosed learning differences.

Identifying Sara's learning differences is crucial to lowering her stress levels in school and at home. As we discussed in Chapter 2, unidentified learning differences are a major cause of bullying because they generate emotional stress. Sara may be suffering from a number of learning challenges, processing difficulties, and executive-functioning problems as well as dyslexia and attention issues.

Until Sara gets a proper learning evaluation, no amount of tutoring or therapy will help. In fact, Sara's defiant bullying is likely to get worse as her hopelessness increases.

Once her learning differences are identified, a learning specialist should be employed to target Sara's problem areas and give her the skills that she needs to succeed academically.

A Full Medical Check-up A full medical exam is recommended to rule out any health issues related to Sara's precocious puberty, which is out of sync with the norm.

Girls are ten times more likely to experience precocious puberty than boys. This results in significant social and emotional stress, often in the form of ridicule from peers. An early entry into puberty also floods teens with thoughts and feelings that they are too young to process or understand. It also can cause moodiness, irritability, and sleep disruption.

An appointment with a doctor who specializes in adolescent medicine would help rule out any hormonally related issues and help Sara to better understand the changes that are happening in her body and how they affect her mood.

Exercise As we discussed in Chapter 2, a cardio workout is Sara's best defense against depression and anxiety.

Sara is desperately in need of tension outlets. Naturally, she'll resist joining a gym or sports team, but her parents could encourage her by accompanying her.

For example, Sara could go for bike rides with her dad, take swimming classes with her mom, enroll in a spin class with a friend—anything to get her moving again. Sara was an excellent soccer player in elementary school; revisiting soccer when her mood improves would be an excellent idea!

Esteem-Building Activities During adolescence, kids tend to abandon activities that they associate with early childhood: They stop playing guitar or piano, refuse to go to dance class, give up drawing or painting. Soon they are left with no self-soothing creative outlets. I encouraged Marcus and Lisa to resurrect activities that Sara enjoyed in the past. For example, Sara loved pottery in elementary school. Joining a pottery class would be fun for Sara and give her a boost in self-esteem.

Therapy Sara needs help developing a language for feelings. Repressed emotions are most likely to be fueling her bullying behaviors. The right individual therapist could help Sara put her frustrations and fears into words rather than discharging them through bullying. The right therapist would help normalize her struggles and open new pathways for self-expression. And the right therapist could also arrange for family meetings to address Sara's insecurities concerning family dynamics.

Finally, peer group therapy would help Sara learn to develop more intimate and rewarding friendships. The support of a positive peer group would help her feel less isolated and more comfortable socially.

The Anxious Bully

Kids with an Anxious Bullying Style

> ➤ Is your kid continually on the verge of a nervous breakdown?

> ➤ Does she need constant comforting and reassuring?

> ➤ Does he torment you with his relentless fears and worries?

> ➤ Does he bulldoze you with high-anxiety demands?

> ➤ Are your kid's angst-filled monologues wearing you down?

> ➤ Does she constantly worry about what others think?

> ➤ Does she have trouble being alone?

> ➤ Is she endlessly seeking attention from you?

> ➤ Does she have an anemic social life?

> ➤ Is your kid terrified of speaking in class?

Anxious children tend to oscillate between clinging to their parents and pushing them away. Of course, it's natural for kids to turn to their parents for comfort, but an anxious kid's fretfulness is exhausting. Anxious kids have little or no self-soothing skills. The moment they feel threatened or frightened, they run to their parents for reassurance. Once comforted, they reject their parents again. And so the cycle repeats again and again.

In their heart, anxious kids don't want to be dependent on their parents, but they can't break free of their reliance on them. They appear less outwardly aggressive than defiant kids, but their bullying—powered by constant neediness—is no less intense.

Here's the worst part: If anxious kids don't learn to be self-reliant, their parents will become enablers. When this happens, the kids rarely leave home or find their own way in the world.

Love that enables ultimately disempowers.

Good and Bad News About Anxious Kids

The good news: Unlike defiant kids who outwardly rebel, anxious kids are too fearful to put themselves in dangerous situations, so they rarely engage in risky behaviors. Parents are more likely to spend their time begging them to leave their rooms and venture out into the world. The more their parents push them out the door, the more anxious kids dig in. Hunkering down in a bedroom is far more satisfying than the unknowns that lie beyond the front door. For anxious kids, the familiar always wins over the unknown.

The bad news: Anxious children have trouble growing up. Anything chancy, anything that involves risk, increases their anxiety. As a result, they miss out on many opportunities for growth.

What Drives the Anxious Kid to Bully?

Parents of anxious kids often wonder:

Was my kid born anxious?

Am I doing something wrong?

Is something that I don't know about causing him anxiety?

These are great questions to investigate. Rather than get caught in the old dilemma of nature verse nurture, consider nature and nurture to get a clear diagnostic picture.

For example, let's consider your child's age, temperament, and family history:

➤ Is there a history of anxiety in your family?

➤ Have you had difficulties with anxiety?

➤ Has your kid always been anxious, or did it come on suddenly?

If your family has a history of anxiety, it's more likely that your child inherited this trait. Also keep in mind that anxiety is contagious.

Parents who are anxious or families that are filled with conflict and angst are likely to produce anxious children.

Though your kid may appear wired for anxiety, there are plenty of things you can do to break the cycle. First, let's look for changes in your kid's environment that could be generating anxiety:

> Have there been any modifications in family routines, such as moving homes, changing schools, or starting a new class?

> Are your kid's social insecurities ongoing or recent?

> Did your kid experience a traumatic event?

Sudden changes in mood or temperament usually have clear precipitating events. These are easy to spot and usually affect the whole family. Developmental shifts, however, are often overlooked.

For example, it's common for many kids to develop off-the-wall anxiety as they enter into adolescence. Adolescence, with its surge of hormones, massive psychological shifts, and physiological maturation triggers enormous insecurities in preteens and teens. Many kids who were calm, cool, and collected in elementary school suddenly turn wacky in middle and high school. These developmental responses to adolescence are referred to as *normative developmental crises*.

To grasp the complexities of children with anxious bullying styles, let's spend some time with one.

PARENTING DILEMMA: MEET BERNARDO

Age: 9
Personality Type: Anxious
Favorite Bullying Tactics: Nagging and meltdowns
Parents: Divorced, single mom
Bullying Moment:

"Bernardo! We're leaving in ten minutes!" Samantha shouts from her bedroom as she smooths down her outfit and grabs her purse. The house is oddly quiet.

"I said we're leaving in ten minutes. Bernardo!"

Suspecting the worst, Samantha heads for Bernardo's room and discovers him sitting on his bed in his boxer shorts.

Phase 1: Begging

"Please let me stay home," Bernardo implores his mother.

Samantha closes her eyes tight. She's determined not to get a tension headache. "It's a birthday party. It's fun," she says.

"Pleeeeasseee! I don't want to go."

"Louise is expecting you. Besides, you know everyone."

"I know them, but I don't *know* know them."

Samantha feels her temperature rising. "Get dressed," she demands.

"My stomach hurts. I can't swallow."

"Bernardo . . . ."

Phase 2: Badgering

"Feel my head."

"You've got three seconds. . . . One!"

"I don't want to go to a stupid birthday party . . ."

"Two!"

"The kids are so spoiled. You said so yourself . . ."

"THREE!"

"Dad says you're selfish!"

This trick always works. Change the subject and distract his mother from the issue. Watch and be amazed.

"Your father said what?" she asks, taking the bait.

"I promised I wouldn't tell."

"What did he say?"

"He said that you didn't want me to be born."

Samantha rubs her temples. Hello tension headache. "He told you that?"

"I promised I wouldn't tell you . . . but, yeah, he did."

Bernardo's plan works like a charm.

"Fine, stay home," she says. "But no television, computer, cell phone, tablet, video games . . ."

"You're punishing me for being sick?"

"You're not sick."

Phase 3: Bullying

"I hate you."

Samantha searches her purse for aspirin as she heads for the door. "Do whatever you want," she says. "I don't care,"

Bernardo screams after her: "I wish I had a real mother!"

Samantha hollers back: "I wish I had a normal son!"

Bernardo waits until he hears the front door slam before jumping out of bed, heading to his computer, and logging on to his favorite gaming site.

Bernardo's History

According to Samantha, Bernardo was anxious from the very beginning.

"He kicked like crazy in my womb, like he couldn't wait to get out," she says. "Then he was born three weeks late. Even then he didn't even know what he wanted. Bernardo wasn't on time for his own birth."

Bernardo was a colicky baby who always wanted to be held. No matter how deeply he slept in his Samantha's arms, the minute she put him down, he screamed bloody murder.

Samantha had never planned on being a single mom. "Being a divorced single mom with a deadbeat dad wasn't part of my life plan," she says.

Samantha arrives home late every night, exhausted and drained from work. By dinnertime, she's falling asleep on her feet. She gives Bernardo whatever he wants so she can have a moment of peace to herself.

Bernardo's Secret Fears

Since his parent's divorce, Bernardo attempts to control every aspect of his life. He obsessively clings to sameness: same books, same television shows, same clothes.

In addition to bullying, Bernardo has developed many obsessions. He watches episodes of certain television shows over and over, rereads the same books, and arranges his clothes by day, color, and texture.

Meals are even more peculiar: specific foods on specific days. Here's a sampling:

> ➤ *Breakfast:* dark toast (no butter), half an apple (no skin), warm grape soda

> ➤ *Lunch:* peanut butter on crackers with banana and a glass of unsweetened black tea

> ➤ *Dinner:* hot dogs (pan-fried, not boiled) cut in small pieces, to be eaten with bright-colored toothpicks and microwave fat-free popcorn (Bernardo refuses to touch the popcorn; he claims that the feel of popcorn on his fingers makes him nauseous.)

Obsessive behavior is always an attempt to build a buttress against overwhelming anxiety. While Bernardo finds comfort in these obsessions, it never lasts. His anxiety returns because its true cause hasn't been identified or treated.

Deep down, Bernardo suspects that his father no longer cares about him. He rarely calls, and his visits are less frequent. *"This year, he didn't even remember my birthday."*

Bernardo's feelings of abandonment cause him to glom onto his mother. He clings to her until she feels suffocated by him.

When Samantha asks for space, Bernardo's pain turns to bullying. Samantha's rejection of him triggers his abandonment feelings—and his bullying.

Before we get to the major interventions, let's consider what Samantha can do right now.

Immediate Interventions

Here are a few actions that Samantha can take right away.

Set Limits Having limits on computer gaming is a must for Bernardo. Unlimited Internet access adds to his isolation and obsessive tendencies. When surfing the net begins to take the place of more creative activities and socializing, it's time to consider restricting access. Without parental supervision or controls, Bernardo is more likely to be exposed to inappropriate material online, which he'll have difficulty understanding. This increases his anxiety and uneasiness.

Of course, Bernardo will have a meltdown when his mother sets limits, but Samantha should not be swayed. She must not let Bernardo manipulate her. She's making a parenting decision based on what's good for her son, not what he wants. For example, there are online services available to parents that time-limit Internet access, block certain sites, and filter inappropriate content.

Once limits are set on computer time and gaming, parents often report a decline in bullying and an improvement in their kid's mood. The intensity of computer games keeps Bernardo in a constant state of overstimulation. Everything in the real world becomes a distraction to his gaming. He grows impatient and impulsive. He loses the ability to communicate thoughtfully. And the more dependent he becomes on the Internet, the less he will be able to develop meaningful relationships.

De-escalate Conflicts Samantha is too reactive to Bernardo's provocations. Rather than reduce conflicts, she escalates them. Later, when she calms down, she is horrified by what she has said. Filled with remorse, she apologizes. And she and Bernardo cycle through the same conflicts over and over again.

De-escalating conflicts, validating feelings, and praising strengths (see Chapter 2 for more details) would relieve the tension of the moment and lessen Bernardo's bullying. If Samantha is feeling overwhelmed, it would be better for her to step away from the conflict, collect herself, and then return. As long as she responds to Bernardo's attacks with counterattacks, there is no hope for disrupting the cycle of bullying in her home.

Household Responsibilities No parent should ever feel like a maid or private chef. Samantha enables Bernardo's obsessions by servicing them.

Bernardo has no responsibilities around his household. Samantha, who is already overworked, prepares meals, cleans his room, and does his laundry. Giving her son more chores around the house would help him become more responsible and less dependent on her.

Lowering Bernardo's anxiety is our top priority. Once that is achieved, other interventions may include the following.

A Parent Support Group Samantha shows all the signs of parent burnout. As we've already seen, no parent can be effective when suffering from burnout.

Before we can reduce Bernardo's bullying, Samantha needs to get more support for herself. The struggles of being a single mom are significant. The encouragement and support she would find in a parent group could revitalize Samantha's parenting, reduce her reactivity, and help her better manage her feelings.

Peer Group Therapy Bernardo spends far too much time alone. The more he becomes isolated and infatuated with technology, the more antisocial he will become. Additionally, his obsessive-compulsive behaviors will eventually become unmanageable.

Bernardo would greatly benefit from peer group therapy or involvement in a youth program. Of course, he'll resist. Too many parents give up when their kids say no to something new. But you can't be a good parent without making unpopular decisions. Without this intervention, Bernardo's bullying will become his only tension outlet, and his anxiety will become crippling.

Friendships will bring new energy into Bernardo's life and offer him opportunities for growth. In group therapy, Bernardo will also meet other kids who are struggling with the aftermath of a divorce. He'll be less isolated and better supported, which can lead to new ways of coping with stress, greater autonomy, and less dependence on his mom.

Family Sessions Short-term family sessions will help Bernardo and Samantha improve their communication skills and set limits on name calling and mutual disrespect. Bernardo and Samantha need to learn how to express frustration without attacking each other. Family sessions would also help them agree on structure, limits, and boundaries for behaviors at home.

Child Support I've worked with hundreds of single moms who suffer with deadbeat dads. No matter how they try to protect their kid, single parents become a target for all the anger their children feel toward the absent parent.

Since all efforts to involve Bernardo's dad have failed, and he doesn't provide any child support whatsoever, Samantha would be encouraged to take legal action. Admittedly, this could be a grueling undertaking, and possibly an ugly battle. More financial support would help lessen Samantha's financial burdens and give her a greater sense of empowerment. Plus, she'd have more stamina to stand up to Bernardo's bullying.

No one looks forward to taking legal action against a family member, and perhaps it's a gamble, but in Samantha's case, it's important that she try. Allowing Bernardo's father to come in and out of his life without offering any support is terrible for Bernardo. Like many kids who are being raised by a single mother, Bernardo unloads all his frustrations with his father on her.

Recently, I worked with a single mom who, after years of receiving no financial support, finally contacted a lawyer. Without even going to court, she received a check for two years of unpaid child support. In the end, she questioned why she hadn't taken action sooner.

Standing up for what she deserves from her ex-husband and demanding what she is entitled to would empower Samantha to stand up to her child's bullying, too!

The Manipulative Bully

Kids with a Manipulative Bullying Style

➤ Is your kid an excellent liar?

➤ Does your kid have a history of stealing?

➤ Does he know how to exploit your fears?

➤ Does his mood plummet when you deny his wishes?

➤ Are you blackmailed with threats of self-harm?

➤ Is your kid guilty of truancy or cutting classes regularly?

➤ Has your kid faked illnesses?

➤ Does she have a history of drug or alcohol use?

➤ Has she been suspended from school?

➤ Does she take advantage of her friends?

If you suffer fears and insecurities about your parenting, it won't take long for a manipulative bullying child to home in on them, particularly if you are an anxious or guilty parent. (We'll explore the tendencies of anxious and guilty parents in Chapter 5.)

Phony illness or injuries, elaborate plots, extortion, blackmail—these are the tools that the manipulative bully uses to extort his wants and needs from his parents by preying on their anxieties and generating self-doubt.

This can make the manipulative bully sound like a demon child, destined to ruin a family. Of course, that's not true. Just as with the defiant and anxious bullying styles, the manipulative bully is trying to manage his fears and insecurities by controlling his environment and everyone in it. Getting to the root of his fears, helping him put them into words, is key to helping a manipulative bully develop better ways of relating.

Before we explore the mechanisms behind the manipulative bully, let's spend some time with Marsha, a teenager who continues to manipulate her parents and take advantage of their good intentions.

PARENTING DILEMMA: MEET MARSHA

Age: 19
Personality Type: Manipulative
Favorite Bullying Tactics: Inducing guilt, doubt, and trepidation
Bullying Moment:

Marsha is a curiosity. Tall and thin, with tousled auburn hair and hazel eyes, she seems to have it all. She's attractive, has loving parents, and a beautiful home life. Why on earth can't she finish high school?

It's two o'clock in the morning when Marsha bursts into her parents' home, startles them awake, and demands a family meeting. Victor and Amanda sit groggy-eyed at the table as Marsha paces around the kitchen.

"What's the point of living in a crowded dorm with people who are obviously jealous of me?" Marsha demands.

Victor and Amanda exchange shrewd looks. They know what's coming: Marsha's going to drop out of high school again. They had hoped that boarding school would make a difference, and now they are disappointed.

Marsha opens the refrigerator and searches for leftovers. "I'm not going back."

Victor sighs. "You'll work it out."

Marsha bites into a roasted chicken leg. "Students do drugs in their dorm rooms. It's like living with criminals." Amanda wishes her daughter would use a knife and fork but she says nothing.

Victor rolls his eyes. "You're exaggerating, as usual."

"I told you," Marsha says, "I'm *not* going back. Why are you so dense?"

Now Amanda springs into action. "We'll talk about this in the morning. We're all tired."

Victor finally snaps: "I'll tell you what I'm tired of . . . ."

"If the school is not right for her, it's not right for her," says Amanda.

"For a third time?"

Marsha knows the drill: Her father's voice will increase in volume, and then her mother will start to cry.

"If you make me go back, I don't know what I'll do," Marsha says as she begins to cry, hiding her face in hands. Amanda hugs her.

"I'll call the school in the morning. This is your home. You are always welcome here."

Amanda hands Marsha a napkin as Victor holds his head in his hands.

"Thanks, Ma."

Marsha's History

Marsha was a miracle baby, born on the eve of her mother's forty-fifth birthday. Victor and Amanda showered their only child with gifts. Though they lived on a modest income, they toiled and stretched their finances so Marsha could live a privileged life.

Unfortunately, their pampering produced a sense of entitlement and lack of appreciation. Marsha has become accustomed to getting her own way all the time. She accuses others of jealousy or malice when they don't support her. Worse, whenever faced with problems, Marsha relies on her parents to bail her out. If she does poorly in a class, Victor and Amanda blame the teacher and advocate for a new class. If Marsha has a conflict with a peer, Victor and Amanda claim she was being "scapegoated and ganged up on." Always, Marsha skirts responsibility with her parents' blessing.

Marsha's Fears

As a child, whenever she heard Victor's booming voice in the middle of the night, Marsha would jump out of bed and run into her parents' bedroom, redirecting her father's anger toward her and away from her mother. Amanda, by accepting Marsha's protection, unwittingly fed the rift between Marsha and her dad, leaving Victor feeling alone and undermined in his own home.

Marsha has few acquaintances and a deepening distrust of people outside of her family. She tends to end friendships abruptly when the slightest disagreement or frustration arises.

This leaves her with few companions other than her mother and father. As you might guess, Marsha has no desire to live independently or move away from home. This springs from a lack of maturity, but also a sense of responsibility that she must protect her mother from her father's temper.

Family Dynamics

By indulging their daughter's complaints and attempting to fix everything for her, Victor and Amanda's love eventually descends into enabling. As a result, Marsha's personality remains mired in early childhood. She never went through a healthy emotional separation from her parents, so she remains reliant on them for gratification and frustration relief.

Marsha's unusual closeness and dependency on her parents also undermines her attunement with others. She presumes that everyone will coddle her like her parents—and when they don't, she feels hurt and betrayed.

Immediate Interventions

Here are a few actions that Marsha's parents can take right away.

Contact School Officials Amanda and Victor should contact the school immediately and find out the protocol for such situations. A family meeting with school official must be arranged so Marsha's concerns can be addressed. It's crucial that Marsha begin to take responsibility for her actions and stop relying on her parents to fix everything for her. Most boarding schools have psychologists or counselors who are trained to handle such situations. Marsha could also benefit from working with a school-based therapist who could help her make a positive adjustment to life on campus.

Set United Parenting Goals The sooner Amanda and Victor set united parenting goals, the better. Their conflicts have a corrosive effect on their child's well-being. Their habit of arguing over parenting decisions in front of Marsha causes her distress and prompts her manipulative tendencies.

If working out their disagreements proves too difficult, Amanda and Victor should work with a parent coach or therapist who could help them stay united. It would also strengthen their relationship, improve their communication, and help them understand how their divided parenting style harms their daughter and triggers her manipulative bullying.

Once the school crisis is addressed, longer-term interventions include the following.

More Social Outlets for Marsha Marsha needs more relationships outside of her family. These could be gained through a part-time job, an internship, or a youth program. Experiences like these would help Marsha become more self-reliant and less dependent on her parents. Earning her own money, improving her social life, and developing more meaningful friendships would help Marsha feel more confident and successful. Consequently, she'll begin to realize that she doesn't have to manipulate or bully others to feel respected or valued.

Family Therapy If conflicts at home continue, family therapy would give Amanda, Victor, and Marsha a place to air their grievances and work on improving their communication.

A central cause of Marsha's bullying is not being addressed: Marsha feels burdened by her parents' troubled relationship. Victor feels alienated by his wife and betrayed by his daughter. Amanda is afraid of her husband's temper and dependent on Marsha for emotional support. And Marsha is unable to move on in life until she feels secure that her father can resolve conflicts with her mother without becoming abusive.

A skilled family therapist would help everyone express these concerns and come up with new ways of being together. This would reduce tension and bring much-needed relief to the family. This dialogue may seem elementary, but without a therapist to supervise it, it may also feel impossible.

Now that we've met the kids most likely to bully, let's spend some time with parents who are most likely to *be* bullied and find out how they may actually be the cause of their kids' mistreatment.

chapter five

Your parenting style—and how good parents fall into bad habits

here are all kinds of parents: strict parents; pushover parents, tiger moms, and everything in between. In this chapter, we'll examine the parenting styles that cultivate bullying behaviors in children. That's right, these parenting styles actually promote bullying:

- The guilty parent
- The anxious parent
- The fix-everything parent

We're moving into tricky territory here, so keep an open mind. In Chapter 4, we examined children who are most likely to bully. Here

I will present three parenting styles culled from two decades of studying bullied parents. They are not set in stone. Rather, they're meant to provide you with a broad framework to understand your parenting style, how it informs your choices, and how it may encourage your kid's bullying style.

Keep in mind, parenting styles overlap. You may instantly recognize yourself as one type, a combination of two, or a mish-mash of all three. The goal is to identify the style that matches your parenting the most and to help you avoid the pitfalls and complications that style produces.

The Guilty Parent

Let's get started with one of my favorites. As you read through the following questions, see if any of them ring a bell. Do any of these traits sound familiar?

- Do you tend to blame yourself for your kid's problems?

- Do you beat yourself up when you make a parenting mistake?

- Do you negatively compare yourself with other parents?

- Do you apologize to your kid more than you should?

- Do your lose sight of what's right and wrong in the face of your child's demands?

- Do you regret things that you've said or done as a parent?

- Do you try to ease your guilty feelings with gifts or rewards?

- Do you make excuses for your kid's bullying behaviors?

- Do you convince yourself that your kid is right when he is clearly wrong?

- Do you struggle with the feeling that you're failing as a parent?

If you answered yes to four or more of these questions, chances are, you're a G.P. (guilty parent). Welcome to a very large (and awkward) club.

Don't fret. Every parent feels guilty now and then. It's unavoidable. You're constantly faced with tough choices—choices you may feel guilty about, and choices that your kid won't like. It's impossible to be a good parent without being unpopular now and then.

As you begin to shed your guilt and gain confidence, don't expect your kid to like the new you. Bullies are accustomed to getting their way with guilty parents. As you strengthen your parenting skills, expect an increase in conflicts, meltdowns, and protests. That's right, bullying often becomes worse when parents begin to challenge behavior norms.

You are about to change the rules of the game. This will trigger resistance from your kid. Expect him to test your resolve.

But before we can design a plan to undo bullying behaviors, we need to take a good look at your guilty feelings. To be an effective parent, you're going to have to stop letting guilt control you.

Meet the Guilty Parent

If you're a guilty parent, blaming yourself feels natural. When something goes wrong, it must be your fault; when something doesn't work out, you're to blame.

Whenever I meet with guilty parents, many questions come to mind:

What is the real source of their guilt?

Why is their inner critic so strong?

What insecurities does parenting awaken in them?

As we learned in Chapter 3, your dominant attitudes about parenting spring from your history. That means that your guilt was there long before you stepped into a parenting role. Becoming a parent just magnified these feelings and brought them to the surface.

Most guilty parents were treated harshly by their own parents. Their parents were critical and disapproving, or held them accountable when things went wrong. The voices of disparaging parents leave toxic imprints that morph into crippling, self-critical feelings of shame.

When parents blame their children, children begin to doubt or question their own judgment. They lose confidence in their abilities; they struggle with fear and feelings of humiliation. And when they become parents, they take these insecurities with them. In fact, parenting intensifies their self-disparaging emotions.

Relentless Regret

It's impossible to make clear-headed decisions when you're filled with self-doubt. When something goes wrong, guilty parents suffer from a bad case of the "shoulds."

I should have known this would happen.

I should have been more careful.

I should have listened to my gut.

There's nothing wrong with self-reflection when it inspires greater mindfulness. But guilty parents never get that far. For them, guilt is a punishing force that blocks out the light of insight, generates angst, and undermines confidence. Over time, it causes them to question, doubt, or panic over the simplest parenting decisions.

How Guilty Parents Become Bullied Parents

Kids are quick to pick up on their parents' guilty feelings. They sense their parents' indecisiveness and lack of confidence. They see their parents as weak or ineffective.

When kids enter test periods, guilty parents typically have difficulty maintaining their conviction. They give in to their kids' demands in an effort to avoid conflict. As children discover that they can control their parents by making them feel guilty, they slowly begin to bully as a means of getting their way. And before you know it, the guilty parent's relationship with her kid is mirroring her relationship with her parents. Just as her parents blamed her as a means to control and manipulate her, so does her kid. She begins to accept blame, just as she did in her childhood.

Guilty parents are dedicated and enthusiastic, ready to sacrifice their own needs in a heartbeat. The problem is that their guilty ruminations have a corrosive effect on their leadership and their children's respect for them. Guilty parents are too permissive and indulging, too avoidant of conflicts and confrontations to provide the leadership that kids crave.

But here's the worst part: Guilt-fueled parenting decisions don't resolve guilty feelings, they perpetuate them. And that's the last thing any guilty parent needs!

To truly appreciate the guilty parent's dilemma and understand her inner struggle, let's get to know one who is raising a manipulative bullying teen.

PARENTING DILEMMA: MEET SANDRA

Status: Working mom with a husband and two children
Parenting Style: Guilty
Child's Bullying Style: Manipulative
Weak spots: Doubt, self-blame, indecisiveness, fear of rejection
Bullying Moment:

Sandra stands on her dimly lit front porch, car keys in one hand and the cold handle of the screen door in the other. She thinks, *"I can't believe that I'm actually sneaking into my own house!"*

Suddenly, Joanna, her thirteen-year-old daughter, appears on the other side of the screen. "You missed dinner," she says.

Sandra catches her breath. "Sorry . . . I . . ." Apologizing again! Sandra had promised herself to stop.

Joanna sneers. "Why bother coming home at all? Just sleep in your office."

Today, Sandra had closed a big advertising account at the town paper. At work, she felt exhilarated. But now, at home, she feels like a failure. The love of her husband, Brian, and her adorable six-year-old, Sammy, are not enough to stop her guilty feelings. In fact, sometimes they inadvertently make her feel worse. Even Sammy's greetings induce guilt in Sandra. "Welcome home, Mommy! Daddy let me stay up late to see you."

Another pang of guilt as Sandra thinks to herself, "Is it really that late?"

Joanna tosses aside her homework and stomps up the stairs to her bedroom. Sandra calls after her.

"I'm off tomorrow. How about we catch a movie?"

"No thanks."

"How about lunch?"

"Take me clothes shopping."

"Okay. Great!"

Joanna has plenty of clothes, and Sandra knows it. But shopping is the only time they have left together. It doesn't occur to Sandra that she's rewarding Joanna's bullying with unappreciated gifts.

Sandra has it all: a loving husband, attractive children, a beautiful home, and a thriving career. Why on earth does she feel guilty?

Before we can give Sandra the tools to take back her power, we have to clean up her *negative self-talk*. Let's begin by applying what we learned in Chapter 3 and examine the causes of her guilt.

An Idolized Father

Sandra adored her dad, a traveling salesman beloved by his customers. She can still hear the sound of his baritone voice singing out when he walked in the front door. "I'm home, you lucky people!"

Sandra loved his gargantuan bear hug that lifted her off her feet.

"How's my big girl?"

The moment he arrived home, Sandra showered him with kisses. He rewarded her with silly stories and special gifts from far-away, exotic places like New Jersey or Connecticut.

Sandra yearns for Joanna to greet her the same way. Instead, all she gets is sarcasm. Even the gifts that she brings home for Joanna produce chilly rejections and feelings of failure.

"I would never wear that."

"Next time, just give me money."

"Seriously, you thought I'd like this? Do you even know who I am?"

A Critical Mother

Sandra's mother remains a sour-faced reminder of disapproval. She didn't support Sandra's decision to return to work and reminds her every chance she gets.

"You wouldn't have such struggles with Joanna if you'd stayed home."

"Leaving your husband to care for your kids is plain selfish."

"A mother has one job—to be a mother. I never abandoned my kids for a paycheck."

Sandra brushes off her mother's criticism, calling her old-fashioned and out of date. But her mother's disapproving voice sticks in her mind and stokes her guilt. Sandra's inner critic grows louder and stronger. She wonders if it's impossible to be a good mother and have a life of her own.

A Distant Husband

Initially, Brian expressed excitement about Sandra returning to work. But now she senses resentment from him. He greets her coldly when she comes home and never defends her from Joanna's attacks. At night, he stays on his side of the bed—and when she initiates contact, he rolls over and faces the wall. They used to have sex regularly; now, Sandra can't remember the last time they even kissed.

On the other hand, Brian's relationship with his daughter has never been better, They laugh often, go out to dinner, see movies together—all the things Sandra use to do with her husband. She wonders, "Has Joanna replaced me?"

Secret Fears

Every night in bed, Sandra replays her conversations with Joanna. She thinks of a million comebacks to Joanna's sarcasm. But the next day, in the heat of the moment, her mind goes blank.

Sandra doesn't realize that Joanna crafts her hurtful barbs to provoke guilt, which gives her power over her mother. Guilt gives Joanna freedom, spending money, and clothes.

Sandra is unaware of this because guilt often blocks out insight. After hurtful exchanges with Joanna, all Sandra can think is that she has failed as a parent.

Recommendations for Sandra

There are several ways Sandra can tackle the guilt issues.

Recommendation #1: Reunite with Her Husband Before Sandra can address the problems with her daughter, she needs to get her relationship with her husband back on track.

Couples with failing marriages cite poor communication as the number one source of their problems. As parenting duties increase, many couples experience a loss of sex drive and intimacy. They spend too much time servicing their children and not enough time servicing their marriage. Consequently, their relationship falls into disrepair.

Marriages require regular maintenance to run smoothly. The more Sandra and Brian withhold feelings from each other—frustrations, irritations, or dissatisfactions—the colder and more distant they will grow. Feelings that are withheld often turn into resentments with the power to deaden any relationship.

When closeness is lacking in a marriage, a father or mother may rely too much on their children to fill their intimacy needs. Brian's closeness to his daughter is problematic because it's exclusive: It shuts out his wife and splinters their parenting.

Sandra and Brian need to work on their relationship by dating again, spending childfree time together and exploring new activities. If the distance between them has grown too great, marriage counseling could help ignite the passion they once felt for each other. Then, when they've refreshed their relationship, it will be much easier to set united parenting goals and put a stop to Joanna's bullying.

Recommendation #2: Individual Therapy Sandra suffers from crippling self-doubt. She has trouble making decisions, avoids confronting her daughter's bullying, and resists either confronting her husband or asking for his support. All of this multiplies her insecurities and feeds her guilt.

Like many bullied parents, Sandra's difficulties are deeply rooted in her past. Speaking with a therapist would be a great relief. She would gain from the insights into her feelings and understand how her guilt controls her. Individual therapy would also help liberate Sandra from the toxic self-doubt that fuels Joanna's bullying.

Sandra may also benefit from joining a support group for working moms. Her struggles are well known to many women; the conflict between working and caring for her family is nothing new. The support of women struggling with the same issues would be a great relief and inspiration. Most important, a group would end Sandra's sense of isolation and help her develop specific strategies for strengthening her parenting and remaking her relationship.

Recommendation #3: Adolescent Therapy What's fueling Joanna's bullying? Why is she such a grump?

Chances are that there are emotional tensions in Joanna's life that she hasn't shared with her parents. No doubt, Joanna is also acting out the conflicts in her parent's marriage. While she enjoys the closeness with her father, deep down she feels bad about excluding her mother. Colluding with one parent against the other is psychologically damaging for kids. Often, it causes bullying.

Brian's silence in the face of Joanna's abuse of her mother is troublesome. Not confronting his daughter is tantamount to supporting her bullying.

Like many teenagers, Joanna is probably unable to share her fears with her parents. Working with an adolescent psychotherapist or counselor would give her a place to vent her concerns and gain more support.

The Anxious Parent

> Do you obsessively worry about your kid?

> Do you imagine worst-case scenarios?

➤ Do you dread your child's rejection?

➤ Do you cling to your child for comfort?

➤ Do you feel hurt when your kid excludes you?

➤ Are you socially isolated?

➤ Do you have a history of anxiety?

➤ Do you panic during the conflicts?

➤ Does your anxiety result in headaches, backaches, or other physical pain?

➤ Would you rather be a friend than a parent to your kid?

If you're an anxious parent, you carry around a basketful of worries that you nurse daily. Your free-floating anxiety attaches itself to any number of fears or concerns about your child. As your anxiety gets out of control, you're likely to begin obsessing and worrying about every little detail of your kid's life.

Every good parent experiences anxiety. Once you cross over to parenthood your perspective of the world changes drastically; you have fears and concerns that you never had before. You worry about your kid. You see danger lurking everywhere.

This anxiety fuels your impulse to protect your child, an expression of love that nearly every living creature experiences. But no matter how much you try, you can't protect your kid from all of life's difficulties (see *Seven Parenting Crises* in Chapter 8 for a detailed list of these challenges).

As kids strive toward independence, worries mount and anxious parents take the impulse to protect too far. In an effort to control their anxiety they attempt to control their kids. They become overly involved in every aspect of their children's lives. Naturally, this provokes resentment and rebellion.

Sadly, the more protective anxious parents become, the more unappreciated and misunderstood they feel.

How Anxious Parents Fuel Bullying

Too often, anxious parents become fretful chatterboxes who over-share their fears, saddle their kids with worries, or express doubts about their kids' capabilities. Problem is, kids experience their parents' anxiety as a lack of confidence in them.

Why doesn't my mother believe in me?

Why does my dad always doubt me?

Don't my parents realize that their worrying stresses me out?

No kid benefits from a voice-of-doom parent. Parents' anxieties can fuel self-doubt in their children, who begin to resent their parents and feel weighted down by their constant angst. To defend themselves against their parent's fears, many kids will begin to bully in an effort to establish better boundaries.

Living with an anxious person can stress anyone out. It can make anyone act in ways they later regret. Having someone fretting about you constantly is a grueling way to live. Over time, it's certain to damage any relationship.

What Makes Anxious Parents So Anxious?

Like the guilty parent, history comes into play here. Chances are, anxious parents were anxious before they became parents. Having a child simply amplified their fears.

Many anxious parents lacked emotional support and sensitivity from their parents during their own childhoods. As adults, they have difficulty trusting others and tend toward isolation, choosing to shy away from closeness or conflict. With few intimate relationships, they run the risk of falling into depression or growing too dependent on their children.

When their kids begin to long for greater independence, anxious parents are likely to feel abandoned or rejected.

Before we go any further, let's cozy up to an anxious parent and see how her attempts to control her son backfire.

PARENTING DILEMMA: MEET DOROTHY

Status: Stay-at-home single mom, one child
Parenting Style: Anxious
Child's Bullying Style: Defiant
Weak Spots: Social isolation, overdependence on her son
Bullying Moment:

Dorothy adores her seventeen-year-old son, Stewart. Tall and thin, with a mop of red hair, Stewart is most at ease playing guitar in his rock band. This wins him many adoring fans. (He's a heartthrob with sad eyes. Need I say more?)

Entering Dorothy's home is like entering the "Stewart Hall of Fame." Dorothy's hallway greets you with dozens of photos of Stewart; Stewart in diapers; Stewart showing off his first tooth, Stewart playing his first guitar. As you scan the pictures, you'll find no recent pictures of Stewart; after twelve years old, they stop completely.

Throughout Stewart's childhood, Dorothy enjoyed preparing big dinners for him. She looked forward to hearing him talk about the details of his day. She adored the closeness they shared. Now, however, Stewart gulps down his food so quickly she wonders if he tastes it at all. Then he flees to his bedroom and locks the door.

Dorothy doesn't like the changes she sees in Stewart. She does her best to ignore the pit she feels in her stomach.

On the morning of his birthday, when Stewart announces that he's not coming home for dinner, Dorothy is devastated.

He grunts out one-word responses to her questions.

"Where are you going?"

"Out."

"With who?"

"Friends."

"From where?"

"School."

Trembling, Dorothy musters up her strength and announces: "You're not going anywhere. You're grounded!"

Stewart bursts into laughter. It breaks Dorothy's heart.

"You're funny," he says. He gulps down his orange juice, grabs a piece of toast, and heads for the door.

Dorothy calls after him. "Come home right after school."

"Not happening."

"I'm warning you."

"Get a life, Dorothy."

It is the first time he has called her "Dorothy" and not "Mom." When Stewart is gone, Dorothy can't stop her tears.

Let's delve into Dorothy's pasts and find out how she is using her relationship with her son to fill in the gaps in her life.

A Lonely Childhood

Throughout elementary and middle school, Dorothy was quiet and awkward, with few friends and a love of fantasy novels. Abandoned by her mother, her Grandma Pat was Dorothy's only family. They lived together, rarely having guests or friends visit.

While Dorothy was in high school, Grandma Pat's health began to fail. Dorothy became her grandmother's caretaker, cooking meals and shopping while her peers went to parties and planned for college. Grandma Pat held out until Dorothy's high school graduation, and then quietly passed away.

Social and Emotional Isolation

Dorothy's one brief romantic relationship (too awkward to describe here) produced Stewart. She, like Grandma Pat, raised a child without the support of a family or a spouse.

Throughout his childhood, Stewart was Dorothy's constant companion. But adolescence changed all that. Now, the more independent he becomes, the more abandoned and alone Dorothy feels.

Critical Self-Talk

Dorothy can't stop her critical self-talk. Even on good days, the negative voices still whisper in her ears.

Everyone always leaves you.

You're unlovable.

Stewart hates you.

Recommendations for Dorothy

Dorothy needs to tackle her anxiety on several levels.

Recommendation #1: Social Engagement Clearly, Dorothy is too isolated and dependent on Stewart. Unless she forms new relationships, finds meaningful work, or becomes more active in her community, it's likely that her anxiety will increase and she'll become a complete recluse, like her Grandma Pat.

Out-of-control anxiety grows worse over time, and it's impossible to live with. Getting Dorothy's anxiety under control is a top priority. Then we can focus on her relationship with her son.

Recommendation #2: Counseling for Stewart Stewart's bullying consumes him with guilt. He regrets losing his temper, he doesn't want to defy his mother, but he can't contain the frustration she causes him. At school, he's even tempered and good humored. But the moment he gets home and hears her voice, he tenses up. Sometimes when she tries to hug him, he instinctively pulls away. On school days, he can't get out of the house fast enough.

No matter what your age, an anxious parent is a burden. Kids tend to feel responsible for their parents' anxiety and blame themselves for it. That's why Dorothy's tearfulness doesn't trigger compassion in Stewart; it triggers resentment.

Counseling with a male therapist could be a great relief for Stewart. Stewart has never had father figure or male mentor. Being abandoned by his father leaves him with an emptiness and anger that he can neither understand nor begin to express to his mother. Every day, he's consumed with thoughts and feelings that he doesn't understand. A male therapist could help him learn to explore and express these feelings rather than bullying his mother for tension relief.

Recommendation #3: Family Counseling Dorothy's emotional neediness drives Stewart's bullying. The more she clings, the more cross he is with her. Calling her by her first name is a symbolic step for firmer emotional boundaries between him and his mother.

Stewart's therapist could also arrange for family sessions with Dorothy, with the goal of reducing the tension between them and improving their communication. No one benefits from bullying; both Stewart and Dorothy suffer as a result of it. The problem is that they lack the tools to talk through their fears and insecurities with each other. A skilled therapist could help them do so and give them a place to work through their conflicts and express their concerns without hurting one another.

The Fix-Everything Parent

> ➤ Do you find your kid's unhappiness torturous?

> ➤ Would you do anything to prevent your kid from suffering?

> ➤ Are you more ambitious about your kid's academics than he is?

> ➤ Do you feel that your kid never works up to his potential?

> ➤ Are you a micromanager?

> ➤ Do you have trouble tolerating your kid's indecisiveness?

> ➤ Are you competitive with other parents?

> ➤ Are you more active in your kid's school than she is?

> ➤ Do you have an inflexible vision of your kid's future?

> ➤ Do you feel wounded when your child rejects you?

Fix-everything parents are truly heroic. They're empathic, attentive, tuned in, quick to respond when something goes wrong, ready in a heartbeat to save their kids from frustration.

They delight in solving their kids' problems and providing solutions. They enjoy indulging their offspring and don't mind their children's dependence on them.

All these qualities seem loving, right? So, why do their kids bully them?

How Your Being a Fixer Can Turn Your Kid into a Bully

As we learned in Chapter 1, obstacles are the raw materials from which children forge a solid sense of self. Each time they overcome challenges on their own, they learn to better tolerate frustration and persevere when obstacles appear in their paths.

Supportive parents allow this process to unfold without forcing solutions on their children or saving the day by rescuing them. As a result, their kids develop the self-confidence and assurance they need for a solid emotional core. Each personal victory helps them discover who they are.

In this way, healthy doses of frustration drive every phase of child development. Children wrestle with simple tasks such as learning to walk, eating with a spoon, or holding a pencil. Every time that they master a new skill, they mature a little and gain self-trust and self-definition.

Fix-everything parents disrupt this process. By stepping in and saving their kids from frustration, they rob their children of growth opportunities and generate gaps in their children's development. In time, their kids begin to resent their hovering. Consequently, they bully their parents even as they remain dependent on them. This promotes an unhealthy sense of entitlement and privilege among children.

Say Hello to Healthy Frustration

Fix-everything parents have a hard time seeing their kids' frustrations as healthy. The moment fix-everything parents sense their children's discomfort, they go into rescue mode.

In truth, they're not rescuing their kids; they're rescuing themselves. Unable to bear frustration and the uneasy feeling that their children are failing, they act to resolve the discomfort by solving kids' problems for them. They don't understand that frustration in manageable doses is healthy and necessary for a kid's emotional development.

As one mother of a high school student put it: "My son would fall apart without me helping him every step of the way. He needs me to succeed."

If that is true, how will he manage to function without her in college? Keeping her kid dependent may feel good to her, but how will that help him in the long run?

Let's observe a fix-everything parent in action and note the problems it creates for his kid.

PARENTING DILEMMA: MEET EDWARD

Status: Married, working parent, first child
Parenting Type: Fix everything
Weak Spots: Helicoptering, micromanaging
Bullying Moment:

Five-year-old Teddy is always on the go. He loves to build and repair things. When the classroom pencil sharpener jams, Teddy cleans out the cylinders. When the radiator drips, Teddy is ready with his little red bucket to catch the water.

Teddy's father, Edward, a financial adviser in his early thirties, loves being a dad. Every morning, he helps Teddy get dressed and cooks his breakfast. He delights in spoiling his only son.

After a big breakfast, Edward straps Teddy into a bike seat and together they cycle to school. Edward loves to hear his son laugh and yell, "Wheeeeeee!' from the back seat.

Today, when Edward and Teddy arrive at school, they follow their usual routine: Teddy stores his jacket and backpack in his cubby, while Edward chats with Teddy's teacher about Teddy's academic progress. Edward greets other parents by name, arranges for play dates, and swaps stories.

Today, as Edward chats, Teddy sits down in the toy area and resumes work on a small model airplane he began yesterday. Teddy's hands tremble as he struggles to snap the pieces in place. It's tough going for tiny fingers! When he finally attaches the plane's wings, he lets out a little cheer, raises his arms in victory, and quickly turns his attention to the propeller.

However, connecting it is even more frustrating than Teddy imagined, and he struggles mightily.

When Edward notices Teddy's frowning face, his heart sinks. He hates to see Teddy upset. "What's up, buddy? Making an airplane?" he asks. Edward takes the plane from Teddy, and snaps the propeller into place. "Look, it's easy."

Teddy turns bright red. His eyes flood with tears. Sensing a meltdown, Edward kneels down to hug his son, who squirms away, pulls the airplane apart, and scatters the pieces on the carpet.

"I fixed it for *you*. C'mon Teddy, don't do that."

Teddy bangs his head on the table hard, creating a red blotch in the center of his forehead. Edward is taken aback. "Don't do that, Teddy! You're hurting yourself."

Just then, Edward's cell phone rings. He realizes that he is late to a meeting at his office. He abruptly pats Teddy on the back and turns to leave. "I have to go. Have a good day, buddy."

Teddy starts throwing blocks at him and yelling, "You're stupid!" His voice booms throughout the classroom, and everyone turns to watch.

Edward, horrified and humiliated, crouches beside Teddy and grumbles in hushed tones: "I have to go, Buddy. I'll see you tonight."

"Get away from me! I hate you"

Edward dashes for the exit, hurt and mystified. Why does Teddy have these meltdowns? Why doesn't he appreciate what his dad does for him?

Edward's History

Edward's own father, a regional manager for a sales company, lived on the road and was rarely home. Edward yearned for his father's attention, but his dad was always too worn out and exhausted to play. Edward promised himself that if he became a father, his child would never feel neglected.

Today, Edward finds himself caught between fatherhood and the demands of his work. He's determined to attend all of

Teddy's school events; yet, he's been missing more and more of them.

Adding to Edward's stress is his recent promotion that requires him to travel on weekends—the very dilemma that doomed his relationship with his own father.

Can Edward provide for his family without neglecting his son?

A Fix-Everything Habit

The talent that makes Edward such a successful financial adviser—being a fixer—is a catastrophe when applied to parenting. In fact, it fuels Teddy's meltdowns.

For example, Teddy didn't ask for help when assembling the plane. Edward may have thought that he was saving the day, but he was actually undermining his son's desire to do it himself—and triggering a meltdown in the process. In effect, when Edward finished the plane, he stole Teddy's victory.

Of course, that was just one small, troubling moment. But repeating these fix-everything episodes over and over will plant the seeds for bigger problems.

Edward's Spoiling

Overindulgence sets the stage for bullying and entitlement. The word *spoiling* has been around a long time. It reminds me of milk that has gone bad. When you repeatedly reward your child, tend to his every need, and fail to provide him with chores or responsibilities, he begins to develop an overblown sense of privilege and comes to expect others to service him, too. When he discovers that others aren't so selfless, he feels rejected. As a result, healthy peer relationships become elusive.

Teddy pays a heavy price for his father's spoiling. He suffers poor peer relations, expects his teachers to constantly assist him, and lacks the ability to follow through on difficult tasks. The more that Edward does for Teddy, the less Teddy does for himself.

Recommendations for Edward

Here are a few ways Edward can begin to address his impulses to fix Teddy's life.

Recommendation #1: Lessons on Child Development Since Edward loves to understand how things work, I would recommend books on child development so he could gain a greater understanding of his son's developmental needs.

Edward would enjoy a psycho-educational approach to fatherhood and childhood. As he studies the role of frustration and understands its importance, he would learn to withhold the impulse to fix things for his son. He could come to understand that standing back and supporting Teddy as he struggles to complete a task is more important than solving life's problems for him.

Recommendation #2: Shared Parenting Edward's determination to meet Teddy's every need is heartfelt but impractical. Edward is attempting to undo the feelings of neglect he suffered in his childhood by overreaching in his attention to Teddy. While his heart is in the right place, he is in danger of parent burnout because, when it comes to parenting, he feels he must do everything himself.

No parent can be everywhere at once. Edward needs to step back and allow his wife to share more parenting responsibilities. She'd be glad to take Teddy to school or prepare his breakfasts. Edward's doting borders on controlling. It shuts out his wife and creates an imbalance in the parenting Teddy receives.

Recommendation #3: Gifts, Rewards, and Responsibilities Although generosity is an admirable trait, Teddy would benefit from more responsibilities around the house, such as clearing away the kitchen table after a meal, tidying up his room, or organizing his toys. Naturally he will resist, but by holding firm and encouraging him to play his part in maintaining the family home, Teddy will break free of his unhealthy sense of entitlement and lack of appreciation of others.

Household tasks will also help Teddy develop a sense of personal responsibility and plant the seeds for caring for others. The more that he takes responsibility, the better he will feel about himself and his environment. Then, rather than taking other people's generosity for granted or bullying his parents for what he wants, he would learn to balance his needs with the needs of others.

Kids need their parents' support more than their parents' service. In the next chapter, you'll learn how to undo bullying by giving you and your kid just the right amount of power.

chapter six

Tools to give you both just the right amount of power

B y now, you understand the forces that cause you to be a bullied parent—that is, your personal history, fears, and insecurities. You've identified your parenting style and your kid's bullying style. In this chapter, I'm going to give you the essential tools for undoing bullying behaviors and restoring balance in your relationship.

Keep in mind, all parents and children are different, but the tools to end bullying are the same. You may swing a hammer differently from others, but all that matters is that you drive home the nail. In other words, the way that you apply these tools will vary, based on who you are and your child's unique identity.

Working with new tools won't feel natural at first, but in time, you'll grow to appreciate them. Our goal in this chapter is to strengthen your leadership and create a healthier relationship with your kid—a relationship that ends bullying by giving you both just the right amount of power.

Your Parenting Toolbox

Early one morning, I received a phone call from a single mother. She was calling from her basement laundry room. I could hear the sound of a dryer spinning in the background as she whispered excitingly: "Last night my daughter and I went out together! She talked to me for almost three hours!"

The mother's voice trembled with emotion. Until a few months ago, her daughter had expressed nothing but disdain toward her. It's no exaggeration to say that she had been completely shut out of her kid's life. Now her daughter was opening up, sharing her fears and worries with her. At long last, a new relationship was coming into focus. "I feel like I have my daughter back," she told me.

And she did—only better. No longer mired in power struggles and control, their relationship was now based on mutual respect.

How did she do it? She used the parenting tools outlined in this chapter and in Chapter 7, *How to Assemble Your Anti-Bullying Support Team.* She concentrated on her personal goals, had a vision for her new relationship with her kid, took responsibility for her behavior, and learned to manage her feelings better. Often, I would see her in my office waiting room jotting down notes in her parenting journal, recording memories, struggles, and breakthroughs.

She didn't hope for the best. She pursued it.

By strengthening her emotional core, she was able to stand up to her daughter's bullying. When her daughter lashed out at her, she remained calm. When she felt pangs of guilt or anxiety about her parenting, she reassured herself by maintaining her vision. When she felt overwhelmed, she turned to her anti-bullying team for support.

Every day she refreshed her determination not to fall back on old habits. In the end, she was able to turn around her relationship and establish a bully-free home.

Interior Work

In this chapter, we're going to focus on interior work—facing down your inner critic and strengthening your resolve to snuff out bullying in your home.

Too often, a bullied parent's internal world is governed by self-doubt, negative self-talk, and fears. Rebooting your relationship with your kid starts with the deep interior work—such as journaling and self-analysis—that you began earlier in this book. In this chapter, you'll apply what you've learned and develop specific strategies for ending bullying behavior.

Throughout this chapter, I'd like you to keep in mind three steps that will serve as the foundation for a new way of being with your kid:

1. Stick to your vision.

2. Take responsibility for your behavior.

3. Manage your feelings.

Keep these in the forefront of your mind. They will take the sting out of your kid's bullying and stabilize you in difficult moments.

Step One: Stick to Your Vision

To begin, you'll need a vision for your new relationship with your kid. A vision will keep you focused during difficult times and inspire you to make a clean break with bad habits. Bullied parents tend to allow their relationship with their kids to deteriorate into endless nagging, arguing, or pleading. They get stuck in a cycle of negativity that weakens their leadership and chips away at their kids' trust in them.

Having a vision will give you a roadmap with a destination in sight (a bully-free relationship). With a clear endpoint in view, you're less likely to wander off course when the going gets rough.

MEET ARTHUR

Arthur had a long history of losing his temper with his son. At six foot three inches tall, 250 pounds, Arthur was an intimidating presence—a fix-everything parent that no one wanted to mess with. Arthur almost never raised his voice in anger; he didn't need to. Known for his icy silences and cold stare, Arthur could stop any argument by simply glaring into his opponent's eyes.

This quality served him well during his childhood. Having grown up in a poor neighborhood in Brooklyn, Arthur got by on his street smarts. He skipped college to work full time in a local hardware store. By age twenty-three, he was managing it. And by the time he was twenty-eight he owned it. Now at forty, he owned three stores and was planning a fourth.

In business, Arthur had a reputation for fairness, but was also known as a person you didn't want to cross. Few people had the courage to challenge Arthur—except his son, Dante.

By age sixteen, Dante matched his father's height and was the only person who could make Arthur lose his temper. Arthur hated to be ignored, and this was exactly what Dante did. Kids with defiant bullying styles like Dante always know what buttons to push to undermine their parents.

The term *bully* often congers up images of a noisy, loud kid, shouting down his parents or pushing round his siblings. But this is not always the case.

Passive-aggressive behavior, a form of silent defiance, is less boisterous but just as provocative as any bullying style. When kids withhold or are nonresponsive to their parents, their parents grow distressed.

Passive-aggressive behavior often shifts the power dynamic in parent–child relationships. Kids discover that withholding feelings puts them in the driver's seat. As their parents pursue them, kids silently rebuff them. This purposeful noncommunication then becomes a tool for controlling their parents and getting what they want.

Let's see how this plays out in Arthur and Dante's relationship.

Challenging Moments

Most mornings, Dante oversleeps, skips his chores, and leaves late for school. Arthur can't stand such sloppiness.

> *"Dante! Wake up! I need you at the store this morning."*
>
> *"Dante! I told you to take out the recyclables!"*
>
> *"Dante! Where did you put the car keys?"*

These requests, usually shouted from another room through Dante's locked bedroom door, are met with silence. Dante can hear his father, but chooses not to respond. This drives Arthur crazy. Typically, he loses his temper in about five minutes.

Though he would never admit it, Dante enjoys having the power to make his father "lose it." Passive-aggressive withholding is Dante's retaliation against his father's constant nitpicking and nagging.

Arthur's outbursts destroyed any good feeling between them. Eventually, Dante began to hate his dad. When he was younger, they enjoyed hockey games and fishing together. Now, nothing remains but mutual resentment and bickering.

A Call for Help

When Arthur contacted me for an appointment, he displayed the kind of candor that he was known for in business. "I'm here for my son. But I think I'm the one who really needs help."

Arthur knew his temper was a problem, but he had no clue how to control it, especially when Dante frustrated him. "My whole life, I was Cool Hand Luke," he said. " With my son, I'm Godzilla."

After helping Arthur develop better self-soothing techniques, we turned our attention to developing a new vision for his relationship with his son—a vision that would succeed or fail based on Arthur's efforts toward self-mastery.

Arthur came up with a simple phrase that steadied him in difficult moments: "If I lose my temper, I lose my son."

After a bumpy start, Arthur's hard work in therapy began to produce results. When Dante ignored him, Arthur sat on his impulse to yell. When he felt his temperature rising, he left the house and took a long walk. Once on the street, he thought about his vision and goals. He knew that a single outburst with Dante would poison their relationship for weeks. This was the last thing Arthur wanted.

When Arthur returned from his walks (he claimed to have worn out three pairs of shoes during our work in therapy), he felt calmer, even upbeat. The walks became a natural tension outlet. They gave him time for self-reflection and stabilized his mood.

One night, before bedtime, Arthur found Dante's bedroom door wide open, a rare occurrence. Dante was doing his homework at his desk with his back turned toward Arthur. Dante would be the first person in his family to attend college. Arthur felt a burst of pride.

Arthur cleared his throat and said quietly, "I'm not going to yell at you anymore. I know what it's like to hate your dad. I'm sorry."

Dante was dumbstruck. He had never seen this side of his father.

"I want you to know that I'm very proud of you," said Arthur. "I'm proud that you're going to college." Arthur left Dante's bedroom, calmly closing the door behind him. At that moment, Dante felt a shift in his feelings toward with his dad. For the first time ever, he saw him as a real person with an actual history and an upbringing. From that moment on, Dante's defiance softened.

When Arthur stopped reacting impulsively, his relationship with his son moved in a more positive direction. Arthur is quick to credit his progress with having a vision: "Clinging to that vision gave me hope when I didn't have any," he said later. "That simple phrase, 'If I lose my temper, I lose my son,' helped me see beyond a difficult moment and keep my eye on the prize."

Your New Vision

Take a deep breath. Take a few, in fact. Now think about your kid's positive qualities. (Come on, I'm sure your kid has positive qualities.) Now list them.

> What are you most proud of?

> When do you enjoy your kid the most?

> What tickles you about her talents?

Next, think of the good times that you've had together—before bullying, when you enjoyed each other's company. Chances are that you were engaged in an activity that you both like.

> Where did you go together?

> What did you do together?

> When was the last time you and your kid enjoyed that activity together?

Now let's revisit those good times and consider how you can resume them.

> - What can you start doing together again?

> - When can you set aside time for this activity?

> - Is there something new that interests both of you?

As you start to develop a vision, remember that no relationship is always smooth sailing. There will be good days and bad. But the more time you spend enjoying each other's company, the less time you'll spend rehashing old conflicts. In Chapter 1, I described how a simple weekly breakfast with my daughter launched an entire new way of being together.

Many parents have found that keeping a simple phrase in mind calms them during bullying moments. Bullied parents tend to lose their centers and become reactive. A simple calming phrase can help to keep them focused. Arthur's phrase, *"If I lose my temper, I lose my son,"* is a perfect example.

Other phrases parents have developed are:

"I'm the parent, I don't have to prove anything."

"I'm stronger than my feelings."

"Feelings don't decide my actions. I do."

Take a moment and come up with your own personal phrase. Make sure it speaks directly to your greatest struggle for self-mastery.

> - What specific feelings tend to overwhelm you when you're being bullied?

> - What insecurities or fears do you need to calm so you can stay focused?

> - Can you think of a phrase to help you in bullying moments?

Let's return to Arthur and Dante for a moment. As you recall, when Arthur got his temper under control and ended the hostilities between him and his son, their relationship improved dramatically. But it still wasn't enough. Tolerance and self-mastery helped, but to achieve his vision, Arthur would have to go further.

To build a solid foundation for their new relationship, Arthur had to find some positive activities to share, something they could enjoy together. Only then would their relationship truly thrive.

This was a big challenge. Remember, it wasn't long ago that Dante wanted nothing to do with his father. How on earth were they going to suddenly pal around?

Arthur surprised his son with tickets to a hockey game. Then they began watching games together at home, cheering their favorite team, sharing the joys and sorrows that sports fans know so well.

Next, Arthur cut back Dante's hours at the store. This came as a shock to Dante, who was again staggered by his father's words: "I want you to focus on getting into a good college. You're going to do more with your life than sell nuts and bolts."

Up to that point, Dante had felt pressured to work in his father's business. In fact, it was the number one cause of conflict between them. The unspoken expectation Dante felt from his father created stress and tension in their relationship.

Arthur's announcement ended all that.

But the real breakthrough came when Arthur purchased tickets for the playoff games out of town. That would mean that Arthur and Dante would be on the road together for two or three days. They hadn't had that kind of father and son time together since Dante was in elementary school.

Arthur's wife, Donna, was understandably skeptical. "I thought my Arthur was out of his mind," she said. "I mean, he and Dante were at each other's throats. Now he wanted them to do a road trip together?"

Arthur split the driving with Dante, another decision that transmitted his new trust in his son. Three days later, they arrived home early in the morning.

Donna was stunned by what she saw. "When I saw on television that their team lost," she told me, "I thought the worst. Maybe Arthur fell into one of his terrible moods or Dante mouthed off at the wrong time. But it was just the opposite. They stumbled into the house laughing! Doing imitations of each other! I tried to get details, but they waved me off, like it was just between the two of them. That trip was real turning point for our whole family."

Step Two: Take Responsibility for Your Behaviors

Parents who have been successful in creating new relationships with their kids had three things in common:

1. They took responsibility for their actions.

2. They understood the impact of their choices.

3. They worked hard on changing negative personal tendencies.

In this section, I'm going to ask you to take full responsibility for your behavior around your kid. Remember, modeling is more powerful than talking. No matter what your child's age, he will follow your example, not your lectures.

The biggest way to ending bullying behaviors is to model the behaviors you want from your kid. Too many bullied parents surrender to the heat of the moment and fail to follow through on modeling. For example:

▸ They demand respect, yet treat their kids disrespectfully.

> They want their kids to listen, yet don't listen to their kids.

> They yearn for their kids to stop bullying, yet they bully their kids.

To get a handle on personal behaviors that can trigger bullying, undermine your kid's trust in you, and get you into hot water, let's take a look at how to better manage your feelings.

Step Three: Managing Your Feelings

For many bullied parents, a negative state of mind is at the source of the feelings that are so overwhelming during bullying moments. When your feelings are predominately negative, it's impossible to summon the clarity and energy that new parenting choices will require. The best way to tackle these feelings that undermine your mindfulness is to consciously redirect them in a positive direction.

I've organized these personal tendencies into a series of four smaller steps to stop old negative habits and start new positive ones. Think of them as a way to elevate your state of life and maintain your mindfulness in bullying moments.

Let's begin with the most important step you can take to clean up your interior world.

1. STOP Criticizing Yourself and START Talking Back

Criticizing Yourself Self-punishing thoughts and attitudes are a central reason why parents allow their kids to bully them. Revolutionizing your faulty self-talk begins with firing your inner critic. That means that you've got to stop letting your fears or insecurities dominate you.

Blaming or criticizing yourself is a form of self-bullying that your kid intuitively picks up on and reflects back. Children have an uncanny ability to emulate their parents' thoughts, feelings, and attitudes about themselves. For instance, if you lack self-respect, your child won't respect you; if you harbor critical thoughts about yourself, your kid will criticize you, too.

A shift in perspective has the power to change everything. When you start to treat yourself better, your kid will respect you more. Of course, evicting your inner critic is hard work that won't happen overnight.

Let's get to know your disparaging inner voice:

MY INNER CRITIC TELLS ME

I'm a failure as a parent because I _____.

As a parent I am terrible at _____.

I deserve to be bullied because I _____.

Talking Back Silencing your inner critic begins with talking back to that negative inner voice. That's right—I am asking you to talk to yourself.

You probably don't know this, but talking to yourself is healthy. It allows you to externalize your battle with your inner critic. It introduces greater mindfulness, expands your ability for self-reflection, and—most important—clears the way for new choices.

JULIA AND THE MAGIC SHOWER

Julia is a mother with an anxious parenting style who just can't stand up to her son's bullying. Every time he yells at her or verbally assaults her, Julia lapses into an apology: "You're right. I'm sorry. My fault."

Without consideration or thought, she accepts blame.

When I suggested that she has a brutal inner critic that's getting in the way of her parenting effectively, she accused me of psychobabble. But, as her son's bullying worsened, she reluctantly began to explore the questions outlined in this chapter. It took a while, but by keeping a parenting journal and listening to her inner critic, Julia became aware of all the critical thoughts that she harbored. Then one day, while she was in the shower, she had a major breakthrough. "I was thinking about the sound of the critical voice I carry with me," she said. "It seemed so familiar. Then it hit me, somewhere between my shampoo and conditioner, that it's my father's voice. He was always critical of me. Nothing I ever did was good enough."

This insight—that her relationship with her son was a replay of her relationship with her father—triggered a turn-around in Julia's thinking. "The more I reflected and thought about my relationship with my father, the more angry I became," she recalled. "I couldn't believe I was letting my son push me around the way my dad did."

At first, her son laughed off her attempts to put an end to his bullying. Then one day, he returned home from school to discover that his computer and television had been removed from his room and put in storage. When he became enraged, Julia stood her ground. She was unmoved. She told him that nothing would return until his bullying stopped. To prove her point, she went even further, telling him, "If your bullying doesn't stop, by the end of the month I'm cutting off your cell phone and you'll have to find a way to pay for it yourself."

Julia's son was shocked. But deep down, he was also relieved. Remember, bullying kids hate to get away with bullying their parents. Seeing his mom stand strong and demand respect changed his feelings about her. He didn't want a parent that he could push around. And it all began with a shift in Julia's perspective.

Julia did with her son what she couldn't do with her father: She stood up to him and demanded respect. Of course, her son's bullying didn't vanish overnight, but he got the message loud and clear: His bullying days were coming to an end.

Evicting Your Inner Critic Start by noticing when and where your inner critic pops into your head. Get to know the self-doubting thoughts that foster uncertainty—the negative voice that you internalized when you were young.

No one is born self-critical. Battling your inner critic will free up psychic energy and allow your true voice to emerge.

Be sure to make note of any phrases or repetitive self-criticisms. Write them down in your parenting journal the moment they pop into your mind. Ask yourself:

➤ What just triggered that thought?

➤ Where is it coming from?

➤ Does it have roots in my past?

Next, let's generate new, positive self-talk.

Inner Critic	New Self-Talk
"I'm a terrible parent."	"I'm getting better every day"
"My kid hates me."	"Everyone hates their parents now and then."
"I'm selfish."	"To be good parent, I have to care for myself."
"I'm too sensitive."	"Who wants an insensitive parent?"
"Bullying is natural."	"Bullying is never acceptable."

Let's replace your self-criticisms with personal determinations.

MY DETERMINATIONS

When I'm with my kid, I'm determined to be more _____

_____.

I will reward myself whenever I _____

_____.

I am determined to change my attitude about _____

_____.

2. STOP Apologizing and START Affirming Yourself

Apologizing Excessive apologizing is a habit that's hard to break. There's nothing wrong with apologizing when you goof up. It's good modeling and teaches your kid that admitting to mistakes is a mature thing to do.

However, unnecessary apologies weaken your leadership and your kid's trust in you. The more uncalled-for apologies that you make, the more your kid sees you as a weak and ineffective parent. Every time that you respond to your kid's bullying with an apology, you empower him to bully you again.

Many apologies are fear-driven, anxiety-based responses to bullying. To correct this nasty habit, we're going to need to insert a thoughtful pause between impulse and action.

MY KNEE-JERK APOLOGIES

I often apologize to my kid when I feel _____.

I always regret apologizing for _____.

I'm disappointed in myself when I apologize for _____.

Affirming Yourself Before you launch into your next apology, hit the pause button and consider these three questions:

> ➤ Is my apology really needed in this moment?

> ➤ Am I apologizing out of fear or intimidation?

> ➤ I am being manipulated into an apology?

When you take a moment to consider these questions, it means you're no longer on autopilot. What's more, you've just strengthened your mindfulness and firmed up your emotional core. Now you can be more engaged, more defined, and more present in your parenting.

3. STOP Comparing Yourself to Others and START Praising Your Strengths

Comparing Yourself to Others The old adage "compare and despair" holds true. When you spend all your time negatively comparing yourself to others, you're bound to feel like a loser.

Too many bullied parents fall into the trap of idolizing others or comparing themselves to parents in sitcoms, movies, or overidealistic parenting blogs or magazines. Negatively comparing yourself to others benefits no one. It lowers your self-esteem and saps your confidence.

Here are some comparisons that bullied parents frequently make. Do any of them sound familiar?

I wish I could be more like _____.

_____ has a much better relationship with her kid than I have with mine.

Parenting comes naturally to other parents, but not to me.

Can you hear the defeatist attitude in these statements? When you lapse into these kinds of comparisons, you're doing yourself (and your kid) a terrible disservice. It's a lose–lose situation: You lose confidence in yourself, and your kid loses faith in you, too.

So when you find yourself thinking, "I wish I could be more like . . ." hit the pause button! Stop! Shift your perspective to all the things you do right as a parent. The only truly worthwhile comparison you should make is yourself to yourself. Ask yourself:

> ➤ Is my parenting stronger today than yesterday?

> ➤ Am I making better choices?

> ➤ Am I seeing progress in my relationship with my kid?

Praising Your Strengths I'm amazed at how many bullied parents fail to recognize their strengths. At some point during childhood, they were made to feel ashamed of self-praise; they were taught that being prideful is arrogant and wrong. Positive self-feelings are not arrogant. They're essential. Without those positive voices, you lose esteem and confidence. The way out of any bullying relationship begins with more positive self-regard.

That means getting used to self-praise. Self-praise nurtures good humor, buoyancy, and flexibility. With more pride and trust in yourself, you win over the impulse to give in to your kid's bullying. You move to a higher plane. You are no longer manipulated by it.

MEET STELLA

Stella felt socially insecure most of her life. In middle school, she fell into the bad habit of "compare and despair," relentlessly comparing herself to other students and despairing when she came up short. Other girls were always smarter than her, prettier than her, skinnier than her. She battled waves of such insecurities throughout her childhood. Thankfully, by the time Stella was an adult, she was confident that she had put those unhappy times behind her.

Becoming a stepparent to her husband's twelve-year-old daughter, Riana, changed all that.

Stella's husband Stephen was a confident, no-nonsense lawyer in court, but he had no backbone with his daughter. He felt bad about the demise of his marriage to her mother and even worse about the hardship it caused Riana. No matter what her behavior, he constantly rewarded her.

Stephen was a classic guilty parent if there ever was one.

By anyone's measure, Riana was a handful—a defiant bully with manipulative tendencies. Devastated by her parents' divorce, she projected all her anger on Stella. Yet Stephen always found excuses to justify Riana's bullying:

"Riana's been through so much. Give her a break."

"Don't take what she says personally."

"Look on the bright side; you only have to put up with her every other weekend."

Stella was stunned by Stephen's unwillingness to address Riana's bullying. No matter what Stella said, Stephen shrugged it off. To make matters worse, Riana was even nastier when Stephen wasn't home; never before had Stella been the object of so much hostility.

"Stay out of my room. There's no reason you should be in here!"

"My dad married you, I didn't. Keep out of my way."

"Aren't you embarrassed to be overweight? I would be."

Kids typically feel safe dumping their rage on a stepparent. For children of divorce, stepparents are interlopers; they weren't members of the family before the divorce and it will take a long time (if ever) for them to be considered actual family members.

Consequently, kids often project their hurt feelings on their stepparents, who may feel like they're paying the price for their spouses' failed marriage.

Stella finds herself stuck in a lonely battle with insecurities from her youth, engaging in behavior she had long ago discarded.

She starts weighing herself regularly and obsessing about how she looks in certain clothes. She even goes so far as to dye her hair and get a makeover.

Naturally, these changes fail to impress Riana. "Who picked that hair color?" she sneered, "I wouldn't do that to my worst enemy."

Stella is flooded with anxiety whenever she is left alone with Riana. Soon, Stella's old "compare and despair" habit is in full swing. She tosses in bed at night and frets about her life in a way that she hasn't in years.

Stephen's ex-wife is thinner and hipper than me.

Riana is smarter than me.

If Stephen really loved me, he'd protect me from Riana's bullying.

As long as these critical voices continue, there's little hope that Stella can turn her situation around. She feels herself sliding into depression.

Stella's story is not an unusual one. Becoming a parent will often reopen childhood wounds. We begin to act and think in ways that are out of step with who we are today.

Stella was no longer thinking like her adult self. Instead, she was thinking like her childhood self. Suddenly, she found herself experiencing feelings she thought she'd left behind long ago!

Before Stella can address her frustration with Stephen's passivity or Riana's bullying, she has to reestablish internal balance by defeating her negative self-feelings. Once she feels better about herself, then she can direct her attention to Stephen and Riana.

Stella took aim at those critical thoughts by turning up the volume on her strengths.

Before we find out how Stella turned her situation around, let's take a moment to recognize your strengths and enthusiastically applaud your best parenting qualities.

MY STRENGTHS AS A PARENT

My kid is lucky to have me as a parent because I am _____

_____.

My greatest parenting quality is _____

_____.

My kid should be proud to have a parent like me because

_____.

Go ahead, indulge in self-praise. You deserve it! You work hard at being a good parent. Turn the volume up on self-praise and down on self-doubt. If you have confidence in your abilities, your kid will develop more confidence in you, too.

Finding a Way Out of a Bad Dream

Back to Stella: When I first began working with her, I was stunned by the negative self-image that she carried around with her. She was a beautiful young woman, in excellent shape, with a sharp mind and striking sensitivity. Yet in her mind, she was still the awkward teen, battling ache and obesity.

Stella, like many bullied parents, was ready for a change. She was willing to do whatever it took to end Riana's bullying.

After the first session, Stella identified herself as an anxious parent type and Riana as a bully with a manipulative style. After our first session, she got right to work keeping a parenting journal. She identified patterns from her childhood, documented her insecurities, and discovered the source of her negative self-talk. She identified her light and dark qualities as a parent, noted her parenting strengths and weaknesses, and created a new vision for her relationship.

Next, we set out to celebrate Stella's many strengths as a parent. All along, she had been very generous to Riana. Despite the girl's horrendous behavior, Stella did not respond to her verbal attacks in kind. She respected Riana's right to privacy, she encouraged her to invite friends over, and she supported Riana in decorating her bedroom exactly as she wanted.

When Riana spoke badly about her mother or father, Stella never took sides. She was sensitive to Riana's hurt feelings over the divorce and did her best to respond out of compassion rather than side with Riana's angry feelings.

By the time we finished mapping out Stella's strengths, we realized that she didn't deserve to be bullied. She deserved an award!

Stella felt like she was awakening from a bad dream. She couldn't believe that she had let Riana (who was, after all, "just an unhappy kid") bully her. But before Stella could address Riana's behavior, she decided it was time for some straight talk with Stephen. When I suggested she bring Stephen in for a couple's session, she replied: "I got myself into this mess, I'll get myself out."

In her meeting with Stephen, she made it clear that Riana's bullying was unacceptable. She told him that he was failing Riana as parent by letting her get away with such horrendous behavior and encouraging her bullying with his passivity.

When Stephen tried justifying his parenting choices, Stella was prepared. She told him that Riana was an unhappy child who didn't feel valued or loved by her father. As far as Stella was concerned, Stephen's permissiveness translated into neglect.

Stella told him that he needed to be more involved. His guilt over his divorce made him not only an ineffective parent but also an ineffective husband.

Next, Stella turned her attention to Riana. Rather than confront the child, Stella decided it would be better to offer more understanding and support. The next time Riana criticized her, Stella chuckled and told her she had a good sense of humor. Riana was startled. When Riana made fun of Stella's weight, Stella shrugged and said, "I like the way I look."

The less Stella reacted to Riana's bullying, the less Riana bullied. When Riana could no longer get a rise out of Stella, bullying was no longer rewarding.

The real breakthrough came one night when Stella heard Riana crying alone in her room. Quietly, she brought Riana a box of tissues. As she was turning to leave, Riana asked her to stay. Then she opened up her heart to her stepmother.

For the next two hours, Riana shared all her hurt and upset about her parents' divorce. As Stella listened and comforted her, Riana's feelings toward her completely shifted. She began to see Stella as her biggest supporter.

It all began by Stella cleaning up her internal world. As a result of her hard work, she improved her relationship with her husband and stepdaughter. Later in life, Riana even referred to Stella as a great friend and mentor.

4. STOP Relying on Faulty Coping Mechanisms and START Standing Up for Yourself

Relying on Faulty Coping Mechanisms Faulty coping mechanisms are lies that you tell to yourself to justify your kid's bullying behavior. These lies minimize bullying behavior and keep you from taking corrective action.

For example, Stephen relied too much on faulty coping mechanisms to manage his feelings about his daughter. As a result, her bullying worsened.

Bullied parents' top three faulty coping mechanisms are:

> **Rationalization:** Justifying your kid's bullying behaviors

> **Blame:** Blaming yourself or holding others accountable for your kid's bullying

> **Denial:** Ignoring and overlooking your kid's bullying behaviors

Here are some popular laments born of bullied parents. Do you recognize any of them?

Rationalization

> "All teenagers bully their parents. It's no big deal."

> "Bullying is just a phase; my kid will grow out of it.'

> "It's natural for kids to push their parents around."

Blame

> "My kid acts this way because of his _____ (friends, school, my spouse, etc.)."

> "Society has made it okay for kids to bully their parents."

> "Teachers don't teach discipline anymore, and that's why my son is such a handful in school."

Denial

> "My kid's bullying isn't that bad."

> "So my kid bullies me now and then. No big deal."

> "Bullying is a form of self-expression."

Standing Up for Yourself To break free of bullying, we're going to need to arouse some righteous anger.

BULLYING STOPS TODAY

I do not deserve to be mistreated because _____

_____.

My kid has no right to push me around because _____

_____.

There is no excuse for verbal abuse from my kid because

_____.

Be prepared: Your bullying kid won't like the new you.

When you take a stand, expect an increase in conflicts. Stay the path! Don't be swayed. Turn to your support team, talk to your spouse, and use all the tools in this chapter to strengthen your resolve.

Above all, be the change you want to see in your child. Model the behaviors that you value.

Of course, there are times when you'll be cranky, when you lose your temper, and when you yell at your kid out of frustration. It's natural to stumble and fall when you're learning new skills. There will be days when you are at your best and days when you are at your worst.

Keep returning to this chapter. Keep upgrading and improving your parenting toolbox. Be diligent and your kid's bullying will soon become a distant memory.

Toward a New You

This kind of interior work requires grit and fortitude. Courageously tackling your own inner demons is difficult but necessary. Ending bullying and creating a new relationship with your kid will spring from a new relationship with yourself.

As Walt Whitman wrote in *Leaves of Grass*:

Is reform needed? Is it though you?
The greater the reform needed, the greater the personality you need to accomplish it.

Next, in Chapter 7, we'll take the final step toward undoing your kid's bullying by pulling together all the elements of your anti-bullying program.

chapter seven

How to assemble your anti-bullying support team

ou're in the home stretch now. Keep in mind that bullying is difficult to reverse, especially if it has gone unchecked for years. In such cases, turning around your relationship can feel impossible.

To go this last mile, you'll need to gather the right support. Yes, I'm asking you to break the silence on your situation, ask for help, and begin to share your parenting struggles with others. Here's why: Being bullied by your kid is always accompanied by feelings of shame. Time and again, parents try to hide their situation. They put on a good face in public while suffering silently in private. Or they view their situation with reckless optimism, thinking, *"This is just a phase. My kid will grow out of it."*

The reality is that bullying must be handled directly. It won't end until you have the courage to stop it.

In Chapter 6, we focused on interior work, such as eliminating your negative self-talk and developing your vision for your new relationship. In this chapter, we'll concentrate exclusively on the steps you can take to gather support in your environment.

Assembling Your Team

When it comes to undoing bullying behaviors in your kid, avoid isolation at all costs. That ancient African proverb, "It takes a village to raise a child," holds true. In fact, it takes a village to undo a bully's behavior. When you're struggling with your kid, going it alone is not an option. So, where can you turn for support? There are four steps to assembling your anti-bullying team:

1. Unite with your spouse or partner.

2. Enlist friends and family.

3. Involve school officials.

4. Seek professional help.

Let's begin with those closest to you.

Unite with Your Spouse or Partner

United parenting is crucial to reestablishing trust and respect with your kids. If your kid bullies you and not your partner, it's likely that you have contrasting parenting styles. Nothing is worse for a child's emotional health than to be caught in the crossfire between bickering parents.

When parents are divided in their parenting, the imbalance throws off the family dynamics. The split between parents can disrupt a kid's sense of well-being and create a split in his feelings toward each parent. Trying to make sense of parents' contradictory and inconsistent communications causes mental stress and a mess of internal conflicts. Rather than enjoy life, they must struggle with troubling questions that weigh them down.

Who should I trust?

Who should I be loyal to?

Who should I listen to?

No child should ever have to choose one parent over the other. It's exhausting. Divided parenting—the number one cause of clashes between family members—also damages sibling relationships. The unresolved conflicts between parents infect siblings, poisoning their relationships and compelling them to choose sides.

Siblings often begin to mirror their parents' conflicts: They'll take sides against one another, blame one another, and bully one another—all lessons they learned from their parents. When parents model negative behaviors, it's only a matter of time before those behaviors appear in their children.

A child's first model of a relationship in action is her parents' relationship. Their rapport—how they speak to each other, how they work through conflicts or frustration, how they communicate—becomes the blueprint for how their child will function in relationships.

Poor modeling by parents normalizes negative or aggressive behaviors. For example, kids who witness their parents' poor modeling may decide:

It's okay to bully someone you love.

It's okay to yell at or belittle someone you care for.

Name-calling or verbal attacks are acceptable when frustrated.

This is why it's crucial for parents never to stop working on their relationship. Married, separated, or divorced, they must strive to work as a team and collaborate for the well-being of their kids. When conflicts do arise, parents should model how to work through them effectively without resorting to combat or bullying.

Let's take a look at parents with opposing parenting styles and see how their conflict produces bullying in their children.

THE PRIVATE LIFE OF THE BAILEY FAMILY

Jennifer and Jay Bailey seem like the ideal couple. They have flourishing careers in law enforcement, a community of close friends and colleagues, and three handsome boys: Jeffery, 15; Ron, 12; and Jesse, 8. In public, the Bailey family looked idyllic. But behind closed doors, there was an entirely different story.

Jennifer and Jay were strong-headed and uncompromising. They also had polar-opposite parenting styles.

Jay fancied himself the laid back, permissive parent. He let the boys stay up late, eat junk food, and play violent video games. He had disparaging nicknames for Jennifer, such as "Miss Boss Lady" and "The Great Organizer." Jennifer hated when he called her these names, particularly in front of the boys. She saw it as Jay's attempt to solidify his image as the "fun parent" while casting her as the dreary taskmaster. "The boys and I would be having a great time, watching a movie or playing a video game," Jay explained, "and suddenly Jennifer comes in the room and starts barking about undone laundry or dishes in the sink. Right away, the boys look depressed. Jennifer can be a real buzz kill."

Naturally, Jennifer saw things differently. Without her management, the household would fall apart. After all, she did the heavy lifting of the parenting: homework, parent–teacher meetings, preparing lunchboxes, and choosing the boys' clothes every day, while Jay—"Mister Good Times"—sat around all weekend, playing games and being as disorganized as his sons. "The boys could wear the same clothes for days, and Jay wouldn't even notice," said Jennifer. "When he hangs out with them, he becomes a kid, too. I tell him that the boys need him to be their father, not their friend. He accuses me of being uptight—in front of the boys, of course."

As you can imagine, the constant arguing took a toll; the clashes between Jay and Jennifer were awful relationship modeling.

Caught between their parents, the boys took sides. The two oldest, Jeffery and Ron, split their affections between their parents. Jeffery sided with his father, while Ron came to his mother's defense.

Soon, Jeffery's anger at his mother morphed into bullying. He'd shout at her, ignore her when she spoke to him, and call her names (just as his father did). Jennifer, deeply hurt by Jeffery's bullying, saw it as an extension of Jay's behavior.

Ron, on the other hand, was furiously protective of his mother. On several occasions, he came to blows with Jeffery and the two had to be separated by their parents.

The split in parenting styles and poor modeling set off hostility between the two oldest boys. As is often the case, they played out the conflicts that were going on between their parents. However, the youngest boy, Jesse, suffered the most damage.

Constant conflicts transformed Jesse from a good-humored and playful child into an anxious and fearful one, plagued with psychosomatic reactions to stress. After an evening of particularly violent arguing at home, Jesse wet his bed, only to be mocked by his brothers.

When Jeffery and Ron united to bully their brother, it destroyed his trust in them. He began to have nightmares and took shelter in his parents' bed at night—the only place he felt safe.

Jennifer and Jay realized that their boys were all unhappy, but rather than work on their parenting skills, they hired a therapist for each one of their sons. Unfortunately, after three months of treatment, there were very few gains in the boys' moods or behaviors.

A Bullying Household

Jennifer and Jay set the tone for bullying in the household by constantly bullying each other. Until they learned to work out their differences peacefully and demonstrate to the boys how to resolve conflicts effectively, the bullying culture of the household would not change.

No therapist is powerful enough to undo bad modeling at home. Until Jennifer and Jay changed their ways, therapy would not produce lasting results. Jeffery and Rob would continue to battle each other (just like their parents) and poor Jesse would suffer increasingly severe bouts of anxiety.

It seems like human nature to blame others before questioning our own behavior. But blame is a dead end: It never produces empowered children.

So before you can take any steps to address bullying with your kid, ask yourself: Are you working through conflicts peacefully? Are you modeling the behaviors that you want to see in your kid?

No matter what their parenting style, parents must unite for the good of their children. This means putting aside time to work out your differences, setting parenting goals together, and modeling how to relate positively even during times of stress.

Set parenting goals together and stay united until you achieve them. Eliminating a family's bullying culture begins with eliminating it in yourself and in your relationship. This is the only way to truly stop bullying in your family. Unity and love between parents sets the tone for all family members.

This doesn't mean you and your spouse have to agree on everything; that would be unrealistic *(and just plain weird!)*. Parenting is full of complications and changing circumstances, so there's always going to be disagreements. You can still disagree to stay united in your parenting choices.

Enlist Your Friends and Family

As I mentioned earlier, bullied parents are everywhere. These days, everybody knows one. So there's no need to feel embarrassed. Chances are, your friends already sense your struggle, no matter how secretive you have tried to be. You'll be surprised how eager they are to help out.

MEET ANNA MARIA AND ANTONIO

Anna Maria, a single mom, was having a terrible time with her fourteen-year-old son, Antonio. She couldn't understand why Antonio talked down to her and bullied her.

Still, Antonio wasn't always that way. There were times when he was a sweetheart—well behaved and kind. On Mother's Day, he would make Anna Maria breakfast; on her birthday, he wrote her poems.

In many ways, Antonio idolized his mom. On top of that, he was an excellent student, on the high honor roll, determined to get a full scholarship to college.

In analyzing her situation, we decided to target Antonio's worst bullying hour: early weekday mornings before school. After staying up late at night, he couldn't wake up on time. When Anna Marie finally got him out of bed, he ran out of the house without eating—blaming his mother for his lateness. "Leave me alone!" he'd yell at Anna Maria. "Stop nagging me. I have plenty of time! "I don't want breakfast!"

Antonio felt bad about bullying his mother. But early mornings, he just wasn't himself. Even the sound of her voice in the morning made him cringe.

As I've mentioned, no kid wants to get away with bullying his parents. Those who do will typically come to regret and feel ashamed of the things that they say. Bullying never fails to damage kids' self-esteem, lower their self-respect, and stir feelings of guilt. When parents let their kids bully them, their kids' unhappiness deepens.

It was clear that Anna Maria couldn't put a stop to her son's bullying on her own. She needed help. When I asked her whom she could chose for her anti-bullying team, her first choice was her neighbor, Greg, a graphic artist, who dabbled in cartooning and design.

Antonio loved Greg's artwork and thought he was super cool. During the summer, Greg would often toss a baseball around in the backyard that they shared. Sometimes Greg would show Antonio his latest designs or give him advice on dating.

Antonio looked up to Greg and turned to him for guidance. Greg was as close to a father as Antonio had ever known. He was the perfect choice for Anna Maria's anti-bullying team.

At first, Anna Maria didn't want to involve Greg. "Why should I trouble him with my problems?" she thought.

At my insistence, however, Anna Maria summoned the courage to ask Greg for help. Turns out, Greg was more than happy to offer support. He had overheard Antonio's bullying (big surprise) and was eager to lend a hand.

After a brainstorming session in my office, we decided that Greg would join Antonio for breakfast on school days. Greg welcomed the invitation. He was delighted to have a home-cooked meal.

I knew that Antonio would never bully his mom in front of Greg, someone that he wanted to impress. This would be our first step in disrupting the bullying dynamic in Anna Maria's home.

When Antonio's mom announced that Greg was coming for breakfast, Antonio was incredulous. "Why does he want to eat breakfast with us? I don't get it."

Anna Maria persisted, and when Greg stopped by for breakfast later that week, something magical happened. Antonio was up and dressed before Greg arrived. And he was pleasant and joking at the breakfast table. Afterward, Greg offered Antonio a lift to school and they left together, chatting the whole way.

If Antonio's mother hadn't reached out to Greg to help, this turnaround would have been impossible. What's more, Greg was also an excellent role model for Antonio. He was well mannered and polite, ambitious in his career, and he had a beautiful girlfriend to boot.

During one car ride to school, Greg said offhandedly to Antonio, "You know, you only get one mom; you shouldn't disrespect her."

That simple statement from Greg had a huge impact on Antonio. In the course of a few weeks, he completely stopped bullying his mother. If he did lose his temper, he was quick to apologize.

Young people, particularly preteens and teens, have a hunger for role models. They seek them everywhere—in school, in pop culture and movies—in an effort to strengthen their own identities. Once they find adults that they admire, they begin to model their own behavior after them.

Greg was the perfect role model for Antonio. According to Anna Maria, "Asking Greg for help wasn't easy. But it was one of the best decisions I've ever made."

Reaching out for help—speaking to teachers, coaches, friends, and others who may serve as positive role models for your kid—isn't a sign of weakness, but an act of love.

Of course, involving Greg didn't fix Antonio's bullying problem overnight, but it was an excellent start.

Next, let's see who else you can engage for support.

Involve School Officials

I spent over ten years in the New York City public school system working with struggling parents. During that time, I discovered that the parents who needed the most help rarely stepped forward. In fact, the more trouble they had at home, the less likely they were to ask for help.

Maybe they felt embarrassed, weary, or distrustful of school officials. Maybe they suffered from anxiety or depression. One thing's for sure: Remaining isolated only made their difficulties worse.

Asking for help is never easy. Being a good parent requires the willingness to put up with personal discomfort for your kid's benefit.

PAMELA'S QUIET DESPAIR

Pamela wasn't a single parent by choice. She'd never dreamed that being an "Army mom" would be so difficult. When Devon, her husband, was deployed to Iraq, she assumed he'd be gone a few months at the most.

Three years later he was still on active duty, with no end in sight.

When Devon came home on leave, Pamela felt that he wasn't the same man she'd married. He drank more, lost his temper, and sometimes slept all day. It broke her heart to see her eight-year-old son, Aaron, begging his father to wake up and play with him.

While his dad was home, Aaron was on his best behavior. But when Devon left for duty, Aaron's behavior would begin to deteriorate. He grew ill-tempered and adopted a defiant, bullying style. Obviously, feeling abandoned by his father was the driving force behind his bullying.

Like many boys who are raised without a consistent father figure, Aaron began to see himself as the man of the house. In his mind, it was only natural to bully at his mother. After all, that's what his father did.

Pamela's biggest fear was becoming a reality: Aaron was turning into his father. Not the good-humored Devon, but the moody and aggressive one.

This was not Pamela's vision for her family.

She did her best to put on a good face in public. She never shared her personal struggles with teachers or parents. Whenever anyone inquired about Devon, she'd smile brightly and show a handsome photo of him in his uniform looking every bit the hero.

Pamela never let on how much she was struggling. For example, when Aaron was sent home for disrupting his class or fighting in the lunchroom, Pamela apologized to the guidance counselor and took her son home without making a fuss.

When Aaron was younger, Pamela didn't allow him to play violent video games. Now she let him play whatever he wanted, sometimes all weekend. As a result, Aaron developed an unhealthy obsession with war and killing, often asking his mother how many enemy soldiers his father had killed so he could brag about it to his friends in school.

Aaron grew more disruptive and violent at school. In fact, he was suspended for a week for punching a peer in the face. At such moments, Pamela felt completely defeated.

What could she do? Aaron needed his father, but even when Devon was home, he was absent.

It was a Friday afternoon. I was leaving the school when I came upon Pamela crying in the shadows of a stairwell. She apologized, trying to conceal her tears. But she couldn't stop herself. She didn't have the strength to put on a good face. Her heart was breaking before my eyes.

I recognized her as Aaron's mom. We had spoken a few times on the phone about counseling for Aaron, but she'd politely refused. Pamela explained that she came from a family that saw psychotherapy or counseling as something for weak or crazy people.

Today, she came to my office willingly, and cried for nearly an hour. It was the first time she let anyone know of her struggles. She spoke of her despair, her feelings of hopelessness, and the unfairness of her situation. A pervasive sense of guilt had begun to weaken her resolve. "I should have never married an Army man," she said. "Aaron doesn't have a real father. It's my fault we're in this situation."

These remorseful, self-critical feelings undermined Pamela's ability to parent effectively. She'd always taken pride in being self-sufficient, never asking for help or relying on anyone. Now she was flooded with self-doubt, rewarding her son's bad behaviors to ease the guilt she felt about him not having a "normal" father.

The more she shared her feelings with me, the more tension drained from her face. Hiding her emotions—masquerading in public while suffering in private—had made her situation worse. Isolation is never a good solution for pain.

Over the course of several weeks, Pamela visited me regularly. Each time, she felt less in the grips of depression. The more she shared her struggles, the better she felt. Accepting help was a first step in ending Aaron's bullying behavior at home.

Next, Pamela joined an Army moms' support group at the Veterans Association. There, she discovered a community she never knew existed. In the company of other Army moms, rather than hide her struggles, she shared them openly. She felt safe and embraced by the women in the group. With their help, she also recognized that Devon was suffering from post-traumatic stress disorder (PTSD), a common condition with serious implications if untreated. She realized her husband needed therapy, too.

Within a few weeks, Pamela bounced back and began taking charge of her life. She began exercising again, took free computer classes, and met friends for lunch. With her new lucidity, she then turned her laserlike attention to Aaron and his bullying. Immediately, she began to reinstate all the structure, limits, and boundaries that she had let fall away. "I can't believe that I let things get so bad," she told me. "As a parent, I was asleep at the wheel."

Overnight, the violent video games were gone and a thirty-minute gaming rule was implemented on weekdays. Aaron wanted to protest, but he could sense the change in his mom. Her voice was firm, and she was no longer afraid to set limits with him. In fact, he was a little afraid of her now. Aaron knew his bullying days were over.

As strange as it may sound, it's healthy for kids to be a little afraid of their parents, particularly children like Aaron who have trouble with impulsivity. Rather than be governed by his impulses, the limits that Pamela put on Aaron's behavior helped him control himself better. The pause between urge and impulse helped Aaron learn to make better choices. Pamela's strong leadership also lowered his anxiety by making it clear that even though his father was away, she was still the boss; Aaron was not, in fact, the man of the house.

One evening, as Pamela was tucking Aaron in bed, he was able to voice the true source of his anxiety—the fear that his father would be killed in the war. He also shared with his mom that he'd seen online photos of the war that scared him. The wounded and dead soldiers' faces haunted him at night. Sometimes, he was afraid to close his eyes.

As Pamela listened to her son's fears, she realized how tormented he was. All the bullying and bravado was just an act. As she calmed his fears, she realized she had to do more to help him.

When Devon returned home, he, too, noticed the change in Pamela. She was no longer living in quiet despair. She dragged him to the Veterans Association and found him a therapist. She introduced him to the women in her support group, and she signed Aaron up for a playgroup for kids with parents in the armed forces.

This was a long way for someone who once saw therapy as something only for the weak or crazy.

Like Pamela, you may fear what other parents will say; you may worry about the family members or neighbors judging you. But when you put aside such fears and ask for help, you become a stronger person—the kind of parent that a bullying kid needs.

Guidance counselors, school psychologists, and other school officials have access to support services in the school in addition to neighborhood resources such as counseling and tutoring centers.

But first you have to break your silence.

Choosing the Right Therapist for Your Kid

We live in a golden age of parenting. Never before in history has there been so much professional care and support for parents. The Internet is full of parenting sites, podcasts, and videos. Libraries, bookstores, and community centers host discussions with authors of parenting books. Psychotherapists and social workers in schools and private practices now specialize in parenting. But finding the *right* therapist for your child can be challenging. As one parent recently said in my office, "The whole process was so stressful. By the time I found a therapist for my kid, I felt like I needed therapy."

If, after reaching out to school officials and friends about your kid's bullying, you decide that you would like to consult with a therapist, here are a few things to keep in mind.

Contact Your Child's School Guidance Counselor

Experienced school counselors have an excellent grasp of local child/adolescent therapists. They can provide you with reliable referrals to professionals who specialize in children and parents.

Attend Parenting Workshops or Lectures

Schools, therapy institutes, parenting organizations, and youth centers offer free lectures and workshops for parents. Listening to therapists discuss their work and explain the therapeutic process can serve as a wonderful introduction to the world of therapy. You'll also benefit from the questions other parents ask. If you enjoy a particular therapist's presentation, contact him or her for a consultation.

Get a Referral from a Trusted Friend

A friend who has had a positive experience with a therapist may be your most reliable source for a referral. Find out how the process unfolded. Investigating your friend's experience will save you a lot of time and energy, and will point you in the right direction.

Choosing a Therapist

To help you choose the right therapist, here are some questions to ask on the phone:

> ‣ What's your background and training working with children?

> ‣ How often do you meet with parents?

> Will you be in contact with my child's teacher or guidance counselor?

> How long do children usually stay in therapy with you?

> What are your thoughts about medication?

> Can I get a reference from a parent whose child has worked with you?

How to Prepare for Your Consultation

Before you set up a consultation, prepare a list of concerns about your child. Bring along any educational evaluations or classroom reports you have. Consider your child's long-term history.

> Is bullying a recent development?

> Have there been any significant changes or disruptions in your family?

> Does your kid seem depressed or anxious?

The more you prepare for your consultation, the more you will get out of it. It also sets the stage for partnering with your child's therapist and working together. Remember, no one knows your child better than you.

Consult Three Therapists Before Choosing

Therapists have different styles and approaches to working with children. For example, some work collaboratively with parents, while others prefer working with children alone.

Take your time and interview at least three. Many eager parents hire the first therapist they meet, only to regret it later. Don't rush. Be patient. Trust your instincts.

Who Are These People? Your Guide to Mental Health Professionals

Social workers, psychiatrists, psychologists—what's the difference? Good question. Although they're all referred to as *therapists*, they have vastly different training and unique specialties. Here's a quick glance at their specifications:

> **Clinical social workers** have master's degrees in social work and are generally trained in empowerment and advocacy. Social workers take a practical approach to problem solving through talk or play therapy, counseling, or group work.

> **Psychiatrists/psychopharmacologists** have medical degrees and primarily prescribe medication. For example, if you're looking for antidepressants or medications for anxiety or attention deficit disorder, these doctors are for you.

> **Psychologists** have doctorate degrees and provide neuropsychological evaluations (see Chapter 2). They identify learning and perceptional differences such as dyslexia, attention deficient disorder, or auditory processing difficulties. Their recommendations could include medication, individual or group therapy, tutoring with a learning specialist, changes in schooling, or additional academic support.

Types of Child/Adolescent Therapy

There are dozens of different types of therapy for children and teenagers. Here's a short list of the most common:

> **Play therapy:** Play therapists use toys, action figures, games, and art to help small children describe their fears and concerns. Play therapy works best for pre-K or elementary-school-aged children who are struggling with emotional difficulties and need help expressing themselves.

➤ **Group therapy:** Group therapy is ideal for children or teens suffering from social problems, such as extreme shyness. Group therapy helps build social competence and resilience.

➤ **Cognitive behavior therapy:** CBT is the most popular treatment for children who struggle with attention problems, phobias, and obsessions. CPT is time-limited and uses a variety of techniques, such as relaxation exercises, personal diaries, and worksheets to target and change specific behavior and mood problems.

➤ **Family therapy:** Families experience all kinds of disruptions, from economic hardship to separation, divorce, illness, and death. Family therapists conduct family meetings to help all members express their concerns and frustrations. The goal of family therapy is to reestablish positive communication and mutual respect.

➤ **Individual therapy:** Who doesn't feel better after talking out his or her problems? Nearly all therapists have some training in talk therapy; however, make sure the therapist you choose has specific training and experience working with young people and their families.

Don't Wait

For twenty years, bullied parents have been visiting my office seeking advice and guidance. Those who are proactive about getting help for themselves and their kids always win in the end.

There's plenty of help out there. Here's a quick review of the points that were covered in this chapter and some questions to help you assemble your support team.

Unite with Your Spouse or Partner

➤ What are the top parenting conflicts you have with your partner?

➤ What steps can you take to resolve these conflicts?

➤ What parenting goals can you set together?

Enlist Friends and Family for Support

➤ What family member or friend can you reach out to for support?

➤ Is there someone you can confide in?

➤ What three friends can you contact today to be on your anti-bullying team?

➤ Is there a person you wish your kid had a mentoring relationship with?

Reach out to School Officials

➤ Is there someone at your kid's school that you trust?

➤ What teacher or guidance counselor do you feel most comfortable with?

➤ Can you attend your school's parents' association meeting?

➤ Would you be willing to start a parent association if your school doesn't have one?

Seek Professional Help

➤ Is there a youth center in your neighborhood that offers parent support?

➤ What resources are available to parents in your community?

➤ Do you have a friend who can recommend a professional?

The Boarding School Blues

I used to dis boarding schools. I thought sending your kid away was just plain cruel—a failure of parenting or schooling. I thought therapy could fix everything. But I was wrong. If your kid's bullying and self-destructive behaviors are out of control, boarding school may be an option to consider.

When a kid has too many negative influences in her life, particularly during her teen years, therapy may lose its effectiveness. Even the most resilient teens waste away under the influence of toxic peers, or they lose themselves in an environment that encourages dangerous or destructive behaviors. To reestablish sanity in your family and safety for your child, you may have to take more drastic steps.

Most of the candidates for boarding school are teenagers, although it's not limited to them. The top three reasons parents chose boarding school for their kids are substance abuse, delinquency, and school failure.

Substance Abuse

If your kid has tried marijuana or alcohol at parties, don't freak out. These days, it's difficult to find a teenager who hasn't. But if your kid drinks alcohol regularly, has blackouts, smokes marijuana daily—either alone in his room, during the school day, or with a particular group of peers (e.g., "the stoners")—there is cause for concern, particularly if your family has a history of substance abuse or if you find that your kid is using more serious drugs.

Substance abuse triggers severe moods swings, violent outbursts, and extreme defiance. If you see these side effects—and you feel like you're losing your child—it's time to take action. Preventing addiction isn't easy, but reversing it after it has become a part of a kid's identity can take a lifetime.

Delinquent Behavior

Shoplifting, trespassing, and other delinquent behaviors typically fall under adolescent limit testing. But if you have these problems, in addition to more serious misconducts such as selling drugs, gang involvement, or police arrests due to misdemeanors or felonies, hoping for the best won't do. You need to get your kid away from an environment that encourages such behavior—and fast.

School Failure

Failing grades, school suspensions, truancy, or ongoing conflicts with teachers or peers signal that a new school may be necessary. Rather than just a quick change of schools, consider your child's more pressing needs first. I've worked with parents whose kids were expelled from two or three day schools before they considered a boarding school. As your kid gets older, the options for boarding school become more limited. If you suspect that the day school your child attends is a poor fit and things are going from bad to worse, don't waste time. Find a therapeutic boarding school that will help undo your kid's destructive behaviors, in addition to meeting his academic needs.

The Benefits of a Therapeutic Boarding School

All boarding schools manage kids twenty-four hours a day, not just the six or seven hours that normal day schools provide. Therapeutic boarding schools, however, provide intensive therapy, counseling, and empowerment programs designed to strengthen teens' core identities and undo destructive behaviors. Choose a school designed to address behavior problems; otherwise your kid may be expelled and you could find yourself right back where you started.

Here's how boarding school can help.

Boarding School Removes Kids from Toxic Influences Once in boarding school, your kid no longer has access to drugs or alcohol, or peers who are steering him down the wrong path. Boarding schools provide a complete break from a world that's spun out of control. Once negative influences are removed, skilled counselors or therapists can begin to address the underlying issues that are triggering self-destructive behaviors.

Boarding School Introduces Healthy Structures Boarding schools provide highly structured daily schedules, such as set times for classes, study periods, homework, bedtime, morning routines, meals, exercise, and counseling. Though kids initially resist such structures, their behavior and moods drastically improve when they are put in place. Such positive frameworks nourish healthy emotional and psychological development.

For example, I worked with an obese teenager who was addicted to video games. His sleeping schedule was erratic, he was failing school, he had few friends, and he bullied his parents. To make matters worse, he had no vision for his future.

After all interventions failed, his parents found an appropriate boarding school. During his first year at school, he lost thirty pounds, became a rugby player, and had his first girlfriend. He was finally on a normal eating, sleeping, and exercise schedule. During family weekends, his parents were thrilled by the changes in him. They had their child back! By the time he left the school, nearly all his bad habits had vanished. He was ready to move on to college and major in computer programing.

Boarding School Replaces Negative Influences with Positive Ones I'm always awed by the positive impact role models can make in a troubled kid's life. I've seen drug dealers become ballet dancers or athletes once they were given access to positive role models and mentors. Teenagers crave adults that they can look up to. Counselors and older peers at boarding school often fill this need and offer kids a chance to make better choices.

Alternatives to Boarding School

There's no denying it: Boarding schools cost an arm and a leg. Some parents spend their child's college savings on boarding schools with the knowledge that without it, there might be no college. Other parents attempt to get their health insurance to cover the costs. If you have no insurance or savings, many states have government-funded boarding schools that will require extensive applications to meet requirements. If boarding school isn't an option, I've seen parents take the following alternatives with some success.

Change of Environment

Removing your kid from a negative environment can also be achieved by temporarily moving homes or sending her off to briefly live somewhere else with adult supervision—an aunt or uncle, a cousin, or friend will do. This may seem ridiculous (I can feel my colleagues rolling their eyes!), but when negative influences are out of control, this can be a quick fix until professional help is secured.

Social Action Programs

Never underestimate the power of altruism in turning a troubled kid around. I've seen teens come back from building homes in hurricane-devastated parts of the country, or return from Peace Corps–style programs deeply changed. Coming face to face with the intense sufferings of others and offering them help may change a kid's outlook. Such programs also boost self-esteem, sense of purpose, and personal value.

Wilderness Programs

Programs such as Outward Bound usually have rolling admissions. In other words, your kid can start right away. A combination of healthy outdoor exercise, group and individual counseling, and wilderness programs provide kids with a much-needed time for self-reflection. Many counselors of wilderness programs are actually graduates of the programs, a testament to the good work that they do.

Rebooting Your Kid's Childhood

I think of boarding school as a last resort, something you try when all else has failed. Yes, it's an unpopular decision, but when you see your kid is heading toward self-destruction or a criminal record, the alternatives are far more painful.

Over the years, teenagers who went off to boarding schools have come back to visit me in their twenties and thirties. No matter how difficult a decision it was at the time, they nearly all express appreciation for the intervention. As one told me, "My life was so out of control, I think deep down I was relieved when my parents stepped in. I don't know where I would be today if they hadn't."

chapter eight

Navigating the seven parenting crises that can trigger bullying

We all want to protect our kids from hardship. But sooner or later every family encounters a crisis that changes everything. Illness, injury, the loss of a loved one—these challenges are universal and inescapable. Every family eventually faces them.

In addition, kids face personal hardships. They may fail an exam, be rejected by a romantic interest, or be rejected by their first-choice college. Such losses are let downs, reminders that life doesn't always turn out the way we planned.

For bullying kids, such difficulties are particularly challenging. They may shrug their shoulders or tell you that they don't care— but don't be fooled. Behind the bravado lurks a fragile identity. And it's this fragility that makes them so vulnerable to life's disappointments. To them, the slightest rejection or failure can seem like the end of the world.

Kids who bully lack the emotional resources for soothing themselves, tolerating frustration, or controlling their impulses. Without these mechanisms, emotional tension heightens during a crisis and they turn to bullying for stress relief.

To protect themselves from being besieged by insecurities, bullies often search for a scapegoat.

Whom can I blame?

Whom can I hold responsible?

Whose fault is this?

Whom do they always blame the most? You guessed it: their parents.

This is why the way you handle yourself during a crisis is crucial. Your behavior becomes the standard for how your kid will face life's challenges. In the end, it's not the crisis that makes the difference, but how you deal with it.

What to Expect When You Least Expect It

Some crisis situations come out of the blue, such as a sudden illness or injury. Others unfold gradually, such as failing finances or the slow emergence of learning differences.

The impact of any crisis throws the entire family out of whack. In the blink of an eye, priorities are reshuffled, schedules altered, and everyday activities are disrupted. As family structures fall away, a sense of unease infects kids.

During times of change or crisis, kids experience a spike in anxiety. In an effort to release the internal pressure they feel, they may begin to bully their parents. Even mild-mannered kids may discharge tension by lashing out at their parents. Any time your kid suddenly begins to abuse you, it's a red flag that she feels vulnerable and scared. Every crisis comes with unknowns that cause distress in children.

When kids can't express their fears in words, or discharge them through creative activities or tension outlets, psychosomatic symptoms appear, such as panic attacks, insomnia, or fight/flight reactions. These visceral reactions flood kids with discomfort.

What is happening to me?

Why is my body reacting this way?

Am I going crazy?

Crisis magnifies feelings. It increases moodiness and volatility. Your kid may have a sudden meltdown over a seemingly insignificant event or burst into tears without cause. He may begin to bully and blame you, or assault peers or siblings in unpredictable ways. These are all signs of emotional insecurity brought to the surface by crisis.

The activities listed in Chapter 2 (such as tension outlets and esteem-building tasks) will help your kid manage his feelings by providing him with a place to positively discharge nervous tension generated by stress.

The Crisis Time Machine

Crisis induces regression. When kids feel beleaguered and fearful, they revert back to earlier behaviors. They might become clingy. Perhaps they begin playing with old toys, or they refuse to travel alone. Others will demand to sleep with the lights on or crawl into your bed in the middle of the night. And kids who overcame bullying tendencies revert back to bullying again.

Of course, childish regressions worry parents. Often, I receive panicky voice messages:

"Why is my sixteen-year-old playing with dolls?"

"Why is my thirteen-year-old speaking in baby talk?"

"Why is my five-year-old refusing to sleep alone?"

Don't fret. These regressions are your kid's attempt to revisit a more stable time in her life—a time when she felt safe and secure.

MEET DANA: BULLYING AS A SYMPTOM

After moving from a small rural town to the big city, twelve-year-old Dana refused to sleep alone. For years she'd slept in her own room without a complaint. But now her parents would wake up in the morning and find her sleeping at the foot of their bed, curled up like a frightened animal.

In the beginning, Dana's parents were patient. They knew that changing schools, losing friends, and adjusting to a new neighborhood had been hard on her. So they made accommodations: they eased up on her household chores, let her sleep in their room, read her childhood bedtime stories again. They even arranged phone calls to her old friends. Sometimes Dana would spend hours on the phone with them talking about the past.

Unfortunately, as Dana's nostalgia for her friends and former school increased, hope for a positive adjustment to her new home waned. She wanted her old life back. She began to test her parents with backtalk, meltdowns, and threats.

It didn't take long for Dana's parents to run out of patience. Rather than de-escalate the conflicts, validate Dana's feelings, and praise her strengths, they turned to punishment. They banished her from their bedroom at night, stopped reading her bedtime stories, and put an end to her phone calls.

As we discussed in Chapter 2, punishments are rarely effective in reducing bullying because they fail to address the core emotional issues that are causing the behavior. Punishments lack empathy and compassion. Often, they're nothing more than parents attempting to bully their kids into submission. In such cases, punishments only induce greater defiance and rebellion. Such was the case with Dana.

Dana fought back by stopping all forms of cooperation. She refused to go to school, change her clothes, or clean her room. She even refused to shower or brush her teeth.

This was war.

Dana's parents, who had a fix-everything parenting style, pressed on with more punishments. They took away her favorite toys, her computer, and her cell phone. Dana's father even threatened to take away her bed and bedroom door, escalating the conflict even more.

Dana countered by brutally lashing out, blaming her father for ruining her life by moving the family and calling her mother a "brainless, stupid housewife."

Finally, Dana's parents decided to get help. For the first time ever, they contacted a psychotherapist.

Beneath Dana's Bullying

When I began working with Dana, her symptoms seemed like a no-brainer. The stress of her family's move had been too much for her: she'd lost her friends, her childhood home, and her lifelong community. This was clearly an adjustment problem.

Or so I thought.

During Dana's session, I noticed that she startled very easily. A knock on the door, a car horn, an unexpected phone ringing—such small disruptions caused her to jump out of her seat. It then struck me that she might have an auditory processing disorder (APD).

Simply put, APD refers to the way the brain sorts out sounds. It was possible that Dana had auditory processing difficulties. This could be affecting her ability to concentrate in school or tolerate less structured periods such as recess. And

APD would explain Dana's complaint of headaches since moving to the city.

Dana's auditory processing difficulties might not have been noticeable in a quiet country town. But in the city, she could be completely overwhelmed by all the noise and movement.

Dana's condition put her on a collision course with her new life and kept her in a state of unremitting fretfulness. This gave birth to numerous obsessions and fears. She worried that someone would climb up the fire escape at night and break through her window. She worried that she would get kidnapped walking home from school. She worried that she'd wake up and find her parents missing.

The punishments Dana's parents were implementing were actually driving Dana's anxiety up, increasing her bullying behaviors and pushing her toward paranoia. Is it any wonder she was struggling?

Dana didn't need punishment; she needed help.

I recommended that Dana's parents arrange for a neuropsychological evaluation (discussed in Chapter 2) to confirm Dana's struggles with auditory processing. I also suggested that rather than punish Dana, they help her find more self-soothing activities. For instance, she could enroll in art class or try yoga or meditation classes at a local community center. If she felt too anxious to take classes alone, one of her parents could take them with her. Creating quiet spaces at home with limited audio or visual stimulation could also help Dana relax after a stressful day at school.

Punishment was not only ineffective, but it was also destroying Dana's relationship with her parents. Locating the source of her inner tension was fundamental to ending her bullying. Once her parents realized that her bullying was a symptom of deeper psychological issues, they were empowered to make more effective choices and get their daughter the help that she needed.

While writing in her parenting journal, Dana's mother recalled how much Dana loved a pet store in their old neighborhood. When Dana was younger, the owner would let her care for the puppies and feed them.

While driving home together from shopping in their new neighborhood, Dana's mother got the idea to stop off at a local pet store. "The minute we walked into the store and Dana saw all the puppies, she came to life," said Dana's mother. "She started to laugh and point out the different breeds. It was a pleasure to see her laughing again." And even though the family couldn't get a puppy because Dana's dad was allergic, the owner offered Dana a chance to volunteer there after school. "It was so simple," her mother told me. "But it was the start of Dana's turnaround."

Once her parents began tending to her anxieties and identifying the true cause of her bullying, Dana began to settle in at school and make friends. Easing her emotional tension was more effective than punishing her. Soon Dana was her old self again, and her bullying slowly faded away.

Adjustments and Transitions

When faced with significant changes in your family life, bullying kids need extra support. During times of adjustment and transition, remember the three Ps: *prepare*, *process*, and *plan*.

Prepare

Strive to give your kids advanced notice of changes. Take your time when discussing the changes, and make space for your kid to voice her fears and concerns. If she has a negative reaction, don't shut it down. Let her express those feelings directly, rather than swallow them and convert them into bullying.

Set up regular family meetings to discuss the upcoming transition and explore ways to support one another. Brainstorming can take the sting out of change. It brings a family together by uniting each member in a shared experience.

For example, if you are moving to a new home, spend some time exploring the neighborhood with your kid. Visit her new school. Take her to a local youth center, where she can begin to form new friendships. Maybe she can hear experiences from other kids who've moved and made positive adjustments to their new neighborhoods. Perhaps there are aspects of the new neighborhood that are better than the old one.

The more you can prepare your kid for changes, the more of a chance you'll have that she'll make a positive adjustment and won't fall back on bullying for stress relief.

Process

As the day of transition approaches, expect your kid's anxiety to increase. Help him process his feelings by acknowledging them and exploring his concerns. Bear in mind, the moodiness, irritation, and bullying might intensify. Stay on course. Don't become reactive, don't lecture, and don't override your child's worries with exaggerated optimism, such as:

"This is going to be great!"

Or criticisms:

"You always worry too much."

Or unflattering comparisons:

"Why can't you be more like your brother?"

Such statements are far from comforting. Instead, validate his feelings, find a way to identify with his experience, and support him. Express your own concerns, too, but be confident in your leadership.

For example, a comforting response to bullying during transition would be: "I know this is stressful for you. I'm scared, too. But as long as we stick together, we'll be fine."

Remember, your kid is on edge, besieged by change. Craft your communications to sooth fears and anxiety. Find a way to praise his efforts, no matter how small. Helping him to process feelings during transitions is crucial in helping him stabilize his emotional core and lower tension.

Plan

After the transition has taken place, there's still work to be done. Expect some bumps in the road until things settle down. Concentrate on helping your kid prepare for possible difficulties that could arise by developing plans together. Explore all the possible difficulties and strategize about how each one could be addressed. For example:

> ➤ What if I get lost?

> ➤ What if I can't reach you by phone?

> ➤ What if I lose my house keys?

Making a plan for the unexpected will empower your kid when problems occur.

Problem	Solution
I lost my house keys.	Go to our neighbor's house.
I feel sick.	Tell the school staff.
Someone is following me.	Go to the store on the corner and tell the owner to call us.

For each problem, craft solutions together. The more prepared your kid feels, the more confidence he'll have when facing a challenge.

Kids love plans. They love to feel prepared, and they love when their parents trust them. When you create plans together, you're saying to your kid, "I have confidence in you. I believe in you. You can handle yourself."

Seven Parenting Crises

Families face many obstacles, I've organized them into seven unique crisis situations that can trigger bullying in kids. Though it's unlikely that you would face all seven at once, it's impossible to avoid them all.

1. Illness and injury

2. Trauma

3. Divorce

4. Adoption

5. Financial hardship

6. Learning issues

7. Death

This section will prepare you to tackle these difficulties and prime you to lead your family through each crisis.

Illness and Injury

A child's world grinds to a halt when her parents become ill or suffer an injury. Feelings of safety and security evaporate quickly. Parents are supposed to be indestructible, immune to life's insults. Seeing your parent ill or injured is shocking at any age. It's a horrifying wake-up call, a reminder that no matter how much we plan, there is always the unexpected. We are all vulnerable.

When their parents are sick or injured, kids have troubling thoughts and worries:

What if I lose my mom?

What if my dad doesn't get better?

Who will take care of me?

Such disquieting questions produce enormous anxiety, particularly for kids who bully. As internal pressure builds, their impulses become unmanageable and they have difficulty controlling themselves.

MEET ANITA AND CARL

Anita was devastated when she was diagnosed with advanced breast cancer. Friends and family gathered around her for support. Everyone wanted to lend a hand and help out, except for her fifteen-year-old son, Carl.

"From the moment I told him about my diagnosis," said Anita, "he looked irritated. He just shrugged his shoulders. He started to ignore me. The weaker I became, the more callous and hostile he was. I thought he would be nicer. Boy, was I wrong."

What was going on with Carl? Why did Anita's illness engender such a reaction?

Carl was terrified of losing his mother. Seeing her body and spirit weakened by chemotherapy spiked his fears. Worse yet, Anita was his only parent. Carl had lost his father in a tragic car accident when he was a toddler. If something happened to his mother, he would be completely alone in the world.

Rather than experience the terror associated with her illness—the inconceivable prospect of life without her—he converted those feelings into something much more tolerable: He became angry with her for getting sick.

Here's the astonishing part: When Anita responded in anger to his bullying, Carl felt comforted. She was her old self again; she had more energy and spunk. In his mind, fighting with his weakened mother was a way of keeping her alive.

In our work together, Anita came to the realization that she had to confront Carl about his bullying. Since her diagnosis, their home had been full of visitors cooking and cleaning.

While it was a great relief to have their support, mother and son never had a moment alone. They were losing touch with each other, and Anita was certain that this was causing him to withdraw from her. She had to create the time and the space for them to talk privately.

So she arranged for a quiet dinner alone with him. She wanted to comfort him, address his bullying, and put an end to the bickering between them.

During dinner, Carl began to relax. It had been a long time since they had been alone together. Anita waited for the right moment, when Carl seemed most accessible. Then she spoke directly to his anxiety: "I know you're scared about me being sick," she said. "I am, too. But we've gotten through so many difficulties together, we'll get through this, too."

Carl nodded.

"I don't want to fight anymore. I want us to be a team again."

Carl began to cry. Anita hugged him for the first time in weeks, and he allowed her. As Carl sobbed, Anita comforted him. "I'm not going anywhere," she promised him. "We're going to beat this together."

In the days that followed, Carl became his old self again. He began helping out around the house and even attended doctor visits with his mother.

When kids are overwhelmed by crisis, there's nothing more powerful than a parent who identifies with them. Too often, kids have more feelings than words. They need their parents to reach through the fog of confusion and give them clarity. When bullying kids feel understood, a wave of peace washes over them.

When Anita was able to express Carl's fears, the tension that was fueling his bullying drained away.

When Kids Are Ill or Injured Kids believe that they are invincible. Like action heroes, they're immune to life's frailties. But it's only a matter of time before they discover their vulnerabilities—a sprained ankle, a broken arm, a sudden illness; such things aren't supposed to happen. After all, superheroes never get hurt or sick, right?

Once ill or injured, kids undergo a dramatic shift in perspective. Frightful questions spring up:

What if I don't get better?

What if other bad things happen to me?

What if I die?

Discovering that you're not omnipotent is a shocker at any age. It's a betrayal of your personal belief that you're somehow exempt from suffering. The first time kids experience their limitations, it scares the heck out of them.

Bullying for Relief For many kids in crisis, bullying provides temporary respite from personal anguish. It provides a sense of power and strength. They might not be omnipotent, but at least they can act powerful.

Responding to your kid's bullying during a crisis, however, remains the same. Don't fall into the trap of thinking that it is okay for your kid to bully because he's distressed. Actually, it's the exact opposite. Bullying increases tension and fills kids with anxiety. When bullying is over, they feel even worse.

No matter what the situation, bullying is never an option.

Trauma

Any unforeseen event that knocks a family off course has the potential to inflict trauma on children. Though invisible to the eye, trauma leaves emotional scars that can take time to heal. A traumatic event might be as cataclysmic as a hurricane sweeping away your home, as frightening as an encounter with a threatening person on the street, or as seemingly benign as a fender bender that leaves everyone jittery. Danger, real or imagined, has the potential to cause trauma. And trauma undermines our basic trust and security in others.

When children have been traumatized, their immediate wish is to feel safe again. To achieve this, they erect strong psychic defenses against fear—such as denial—that creates the illusion that they're unaffected by the traumatic event. It can takes weeks, months, or even years for the negative effects of the trauma to surface in some kids.

As bullying kids strive to distance themselves from the uncertainties and fears that they feel inside, be sure not to punish or reprimand them after a trauma. It will only escalate anxiety and fuel conflicts.

For example:

After a Traumatic Event

Do	Don't
Let your kid take comfort in familiar activities.	Push for discussion of the trauma.
Allow your kid to have personal time.	Force your kid to be social.
Let your kid know you are available.	Overshare your own fears and insecurities.
Respect your kid's emotional process.	Lecture or offer unsolicited advice.

Bullying kids need time to regain emotional balance after a traumatic event. Don't force them to confront feelings prematurely or they will feel intruded upon and respond in anger. Take your time and maintain a gentle touch. Kids are more likely to feel comforted when you respect their feelings. When your kids feel understood by you, they are more likely to turn to you for help and less likely to bully.

Divorce

For generations, divorce got a bad rap: It tarnished your family's reputation. Divorcees were judged harshly publically and privately. They were often accused of being selfish and putting their own needs before their children's.

The message was clear: Keep your family intact, no matter what.

According to recent statistics, there is a divorce in America every thirteen seconds. That's over 45,000 divorces a week! With nearly half of all marriages in the United States ending in divorce, you may argue, and rightfully so, that we have gone too far—that many parents split without attempting the hard work of marriage.

Yet for many children who live day in and day out with warring parents, divorce is a saving grace. They actually express relief when their parents separate. And why shouldn't they? When parents are in constant conflict, kids suffer the most. They feel humiliated and betrayed by their parents. Parents are supposed to model how to live a happy and fulfilling life. Instead, here they are bullying each other.

Couples in troubled marriages often put their kids in therapy, when it's actually the parents who need to be there. Parents who are at war with each other create a family culture of bullying that even the most skilled therapists can't undo.

A therapy session is one hour a week. Children spend the other 167 hours with their parents. Undoing the trauma and damage caused to a child by warring parents feels impossible. Is it any surprise that children in bullying households turn into bullies themselves?

Rather than feeling comforted by their parents, kids begin to feel on edge and tense around them. The war between their parents takes root in their minds, depriving them of internal peace.

At the root of their distrust is a profound lack of hope. When parents fail to model a healthy relationship or how to work through conflicts effectively, it drains the joy out of their kids' childhoods, turning them into pessimists who will grow old before their time.

For some kids, bullying is an effort to disrupt this dehumanizing process. Often, when a kid bullies his battling parents, he is trying to get their attention. He is also trying to prevent them from continuing to hurt each other. In a sense, he unites his parents by giving them something else to focus on: his bullying behavior.

So if your marriage is in turmoil and your kid starts to bully, it's very likely that the two are related. In other words, it's time to get some help for you and your spouse.

Couples Therapy The goal of couples therapy is simple: to restore communication and reestablish intimacy. Couples counseling works best when it helps parents resolve their conflicts without resorting to emotional warfare. It also gives parents a place to work through their differences rather than expose their kids to ongoing conflicts. In fact, the number one reason couples report for seeking counseling is pretty simple: poor communication.

Gather trustworthy recommendations, take your time, and interview two or three therapists before you decide. Make sure you both agree on the choice. Then the real work begins.

If a break-up is inevitable, here are a few tips for talking with your kid about the impending divorce. There are plenty of great books available about divorce, but here are a few quick dos and don'ts.

DOS AND DON'TS OF DIVORCE

Don't: Complain about your spouse to your kid.
Do: Make it clear that your marriage problems are for you and your spouse to work out.

Don't: Tell your kid that nothing will change; divorce changes everything.
Do: Express sadness and regret; it is appropriate to mourn the end of a marriage.

Don't: *Overshare private information with your kid. Keep your boundaries.*

Do: *Allow your child to ask questions and express concerns.*

Don't: *Punish your kid for being angry or sad about the impending divorce.*

Do: *Respect your kid's feelings and give him space to process what's happening.*

Don't: *Work out the details of your separation with your kid.*

Do: *Work with a mediator to find mutually agreeable solutions.*

Adoption

Adoption isn't a crisis. However, it does come with certain built-in challenges. Adopted kids go through the same struggles, developmental challenges, and test periods as every other kid. And bullying appears just as often in biologically linked families as in families with adopted children.

However, adopted kids have the extra burden of sorting out a complicated past filled with unknowns.

Why did my birth parents give me up?

Do I look like my birth parents?

Do I have brothers or sisters? Will I ever meet them?

Parents face difficult choices in responding to these questions.

➤ How much should I reveal?

➤ Should my kid have contact with his birth parents?

➤ When is it appropriate to share information about them?

When adopted kids turn to bullying, it may be driven by the internal tension created by the unknowns in their lives. Often, adopted kids feel caught between two powerful wishes: the wish to know about their birth family and the wish not to know.

This conflict raises anxiety and stirs anger. As always, when kids have difficulty processing their feelings, and tension and stress builds, they dump it on their parents.

Look for hurtful zingers from adopted kids when faced with a crisis, such as:

"I don't have to listen to you. You're not my real mother."

"You didn't have me—you bought me."

"You just want to keep me from knowing the truth."

These statements are designed to hurt and test you. What's the hidden message in their pushing you away? What are they really saying?

"Will you stop loving me?"

"Will you abandon me like my birth parents did?"

"If I mistreat you, will you get rid of me, too?"

Do not tolerate such assaults on your parenting—and don't respond defensively. Some weak responses that I've heard to such attacks are:

"Well, legally, I am your parent."

"I may not be your parent but you have to listen to me."

"I am responsible for you until you are eighteen."

Instead, try a strong emotional response, such as:

"No matter who gave birth to you, I am your parent."

"I raise you, I care for you, and I will never stop loving you."

"I'm glad that you're curious about your birth parents. So am I."

All kids—adopted or not—test their parents' love. Adopted kids struggle with feelings of being unwanted. A declaration of love and acceptance beats the heck out of a rationalization. As your adopted kid struggles with identity, he needs to know that you will stand by him.

So when your adopted kid begins to bully you, the rules of bullying stay the same. Respond with absolute conviction.

Financial Instability

As daily expenses add up, parents may find themselves wondering, "Where did all our money go?" Add to that the high cost of tuition, medical expenses, housing, and more, and there are plenty of reasons for parents to feel financially frazzled.

Parenting creates financial demands that you never see coming. Even in a healthy economy, the high cost of raising a family is alarming.

When finances go from bad to worse—a layoff, a failed business venture, a tanked investment—it strikes at the heart of parents' insecurities. It can literally hit them where they live. A major function of parenting is to provide for and protect our kids. When financial hardships challenge our ability to do that, no matter how parents try to hide their concerns, bullying kids pick up on their parents' anxiety.

As financial troubles mount, uncomfortable decisions have to be made:

> ➤ Should we share our financial struggles with our children?

> ➤ Will such information be harmful or helpful?

> ➤ Will they feel burdened by knowing?

Parents react differently to financial crises. Some choose to hide their struggles; others overshare. The decision whether or not to share is more complicated when you have a bullying child.

For some bullies, financial hardships provide more fuel for abuse. It's no surprise that bullied parents often choose to withhold information and avoid inciting their bullying child's wrath.

However, shielding kids from the realities of financial crisis is a mistake. Kids shouldn't feel that their parents have unlimited means, nor should they feel their family is on the brink of ruin.

The tools for gathering support outlined in Chapter 7 apply here, too. There is no need to stray from the course, no matter what your bank account.

As with every crisis, it's how you face it that counts. Financial challenges are nothing to be ashamed of. Pulling the family together in the face of financial crisis and sharing the urgency of the situation with them is an act of respect. A financial crisis, managed correctly by parents, can unite a family.

When kids are employed in helping the family recover from financial challenges, they feel a sense of responsibility and ownership for their family's future. It fortifies them to know that they can contribute.

One child I worked with went from blaming his parents to lending a helping hand. Learning of the family's financial challenges was sobering. It filled him with an urge to participate more and help out. He sold toys that he no longer played with and began to deliver newspapers and pay for his own school lunch. It awakened in him a sense of mission and responsibility.

The respect his parents showed him by mindfully sharing their financial struggles produced a sense of respect in him. He lost interest in bullying because the situation called for everyone in the family to work together. This empowered him to make better choices.

Learning Issues

Imagine working at a job that you can't do well. No matter how hard you try, you just can't succeed.

Now imagine that your coworkers and boss constantly criticized you.

"Why are you taking so long to finish?"

"What's the matter with you?"

"Why aren't you applying yourself?"

How would you feel? Demoralized, right? Fatigue and apathy would set in. Eventually, you'd stop caring.

It's the same for kids with undiagnosed learning issues. It's a quiet crisis, but no less disruptive and alarming than others.

No matter how they try, kids with learning differences just can't seem to succeed. Feeling like a failure in school is an unbearable hardship. Some children start to bully because they can't stand the feelings of disappointment they live with on a daily basis.

As we learned in Chapter 2, undiagnosed learning problems are a common cause of bullying because of the chronic tension that they produce in children. Poor academics also have an injurious effect on a kid's sense of self-worth. Difficulties such as slow processing speed, poor executive functioning, or attention deficient disorder may be hard to spot, but they eat away at a kid's trust in himself.

Kids with undiagnosed learning differences are constantly asked to work at speeds at which they can't function. They're expected to complete class work that they don't understand. They begin to feel like failures, in school and in life. Eventually, overwrought and beaten down, they turn to bullying for relief.

A neuropsychological evaluation will help identify your kid's struggles and put her on the road to recovery. Once her struggles are identified, she'll receive academic accommodations and support in school. Regardless of learning style, every kid needs to feel successful academically.

So if your kid struggles with schoolwork, it's time to end everyone's suffering and get a neuropsychological evaluation. Therapy or counseling will offer relief to distraught kids, but it won't budge the learning problems that generate chronic stress.

Death

Death is never fair, timely, or well planned. Even an impending death after a long illness can be staggering.

Families confront death differently, based on their family culture. All cultures have rituals around death—communal structures for families to gather, grieve, and process their loss. Families without any particular religious affiliation may hold personal ceremonies and honor the deceased with family gatherings or celebrations. Coming together with your family and loved ones is an integral part of the healing.

Parents have the choice of whether or not to include their kids in memorials or funerals. The decision typically reflects the parents' feelings about death. No matter how much you may want to shield your children from the harsh reality of death, it's an unavoidable part of life. Sooner or later, death visits every family.

Helping kids honor and process feelings of loss and sadness prepares them for facing inevitable losses in the future. Excluding children from the rituals surrounding death, particularly kids who bully, often leads to complicated bereavement.

MEET SCOTT AND SIMONE

I recall working with two teens who had each suffered the loss of their father. One child, Scott, was included in his father's funeral and memorial. He had been encouraged to share his feelings about losing his dad through writing, artwork, and discussion.

When Scott joined one of my teen groups, he openly discussed his father's death. He answered members' questions and shared his feelings. The group members were moved by his honesty and courage.

Another teenager, Simone, had been excluded from her father's funeral and memorial. In fact, the details surrounding his death were never discussed with her. Instead, she was sent away to a cousin's home while her immediate family mourned.

Simone got the message that it's better to hide your feelings than share them openly. When she cried, it was into her pillow at night. Death was taboo, not to be discussed or mentioned for fear of upsetting her mother.

As Simone learned to swallow her sadness, a deep anger emerged. She began a startling shift in her personality, becoming darker, losing interest in school, and beginning to bully her mother. In her teen years, Simone found temporary relief from her grief in drugs and alcohol.

Two life-altering deaths. Two very different outcomes. It is no exaggeration to say that the way Scott and Simone's families managed feelings around death altered the course of their children's lives.

To Include or Not to Include Temperament and age play a big part in deciding how much to include your kid in your family's grieving process. For example, a small child might not be able to sit through a funeral or memorial service. It may be best to discuss the death alone with her and answer questions.

I haven't met a teenager who wasn't preoccupied with death at some point. It's a common response to adolescence, symbolizing the loss of innocence or the realization that parents are not omnipotent beings. Though most teens are generally very uncomfortable in memorial services, parents should do their best to involve them. Including them in such customs will help them to face death and honor their sadness.

Throughout the process, difficult parenting decisions are plentiful.

Should I force my daughter to come to a funeral even if she doesn't want to?

Is my kid too young to attend a viewing?

Should I share my personal feelings about death?

Though these are deeply personal issues, I'd like to explore different ways of approaching the subject of death with a child who bullies.

Talking About Death Kids with a history of bullying tend to suppress feelings of vulnerability. They don't want to talk about death; they don't want to grieve. In an attempt to escape the sadness that they feel, they will strive to reestablish normality. They may binge on computer games, cable shows, or movies. Or they may lose themselves in sports, academics, or peer activities. Some withdraw from the world and hide behind locked bedroom doors. Like Simone, they may try to numb the pain of loss with drugs or alcohol. They engage in these behaviors to avoid the fear and hopelessness that threatens to engulf them.

Never force bullying kids to share feelings about the deceased. If you do, they are likely to bully even more. They don't have the tools to express their devastation. Initially, it's best to respect their need for privacy, offer support, and resist the urge to press them into talking. Everyone recovers from loss at a different pace. Bereavement can't be rushed.

If you have a bullying kid, you need to be especially patient. While grieving, remember to call on your support team and increase your self-care. All these efforts will help you remain firm in your leadership and intolerant of bullying behavior, even during times of loss.

When I told my wife that I was writing about how parents help their kids face death, she told me that she never forgot seeing her father cry at her grandfather's memorial. Though it was upsetting, she found comfort in her father's tears. Normally, he would hide such feelings. Seeing him express his sadness moved her. She felt that he had given her permission to feel sad and cry openly, too.

Sharing your own feelings of sadness and expressing your heart-break about death is a poignant moment in parenting. Your kid will feel uncomfortable, but it's a far better model than denial or stoicism. While this is hard for any parent, it allows your child to feel closer to you and included in an important family moment. Parents that openly grieve and express their sadness make it possible for kids to express their sadness, too, rather than defend against it through bullying.

Death of Parent Is there anything more devastating than the loss of a parent?

You never feel more alone than after your parent is gone. It's impossible to escape the inner turmoil. Home is less secure. Places once comforting and warm are suddenly filled with a crushing sadness. Children who were good natured and cooperative may grow dark and irritable. Sometimes bullying behaviors spring up overnight.

With no tools to process death, kids grow despondent. Many stop attending school or withdraw from friends. Deep down, under their sadness, is a simmering anger at the unfairness of death. In movies or television shows, death isn't so final. In real life, there is no such option.

After the death of a spouse or partner, the surviving parent is likely to get a double dose of bullying. This is particularly difficult because the surviving parent is also mourning and struggling with loss. This is the time to mobilize as much support as possible. Review the tools in Chapters 6 and 7. Let school officials know, reach out to family and friends, find a support group, have your kid participate in a bereavement group or a youth program—anything to keep you both from falling into isolation and cutting yourselves off from the world.

➤ ➤ ➤

When parents are faced with a crisis, they need to show leadership. Kids need parents to demonstrate the hope and strength to weather emotional injuries. That doesn't mean that you hide your feelings or pretend to be unaffected by crisis. On the contrary, sharing your feelings and processing the event with your kid is a must. Even if your bullying kid doesn't respond, he will respect your openness and eventually follow your example.

There is a time and a place for families to pull together and process crisis together. In the end, uniting as a family is the best means of recovery and the most expedient way to heal.

Make Parenting a Pleasure Again

For twenty years, stressed-out parents have been passing through my office and attending my parenting workshops. Throughout this book I have attempted to highlight their concerns and their questions as well as my advice to them. I'd like to conclude with the three most pressing concerns that parents have expressed to me:

How Can I Be Successful as a Parent?

Simply put, the best parents are always growing. A commitment to ongoing personal growth and inner transformation is vital to good parenting. Parents who continue to work on themselves rarely fall victim to outdated parenting models or repeat the mistakes of previous generations. They seldom suffer self-neglect or burnout; they recognize that their personal growth is intrinsically linked to their child's growth; they create a culture of self-improvement in their family that inspires their children to keep striving.

Such parents are also able to shake off the shackles of their personal histories and live more fully in the moment. This is the most effective way to parent. When parents can be in the moment with their kids, they never lose their own youthfulness; they live with a sense of appreciation, curiosity, and openness that appeals to children and keeps them close.

Why Do I Struggle So Much with My Kid?

You can't take the struggle out of parenting—it's built in. The real question is, how much we are willing to challenge ourselves? All parents are amateurs in the beginning; everything we learn, we learn the hard way.

Parenting is frequently a lonely battle. At times, you are a hero to your child, and at other times you are the enemy. In the blink of an eye, you go from being the master of your own universe to the victim of some cruel joke of destiny.

Raising a child is unpredictable. It's the ultimate learn-as-you-go experience. Naturally, you're going to struggle. As you enter the wild, unexplored jungle of child rearing, you're bound to feel lost or have regrets. Parenting is an emotional and psychological workout. My hope is that this book can serve as a training ground for new skills and a roadmap back to sanity when you fear you've nearly lost all your marbles.

What Is the Best Parenting Quality?

Mindfulness is not a word often associated with parenting. Neither is self-mastery. But without either, it's impossible to have a healthy relationship with your child. When parents model the behaviors they want to see in their kids, they lead the way to better communication and a better relationship. Parents teach values through their behavior, not their words.

For example, as we've seen throughout this book, hotheads rarely have good relationships with their kids. My worst and most painful memories as a parent are of times when I was impatient. The moment that I stopped straining to mold my kid into someone else and focused on changing my own problem behavior (beginning with having more patience, of course), our relationship moved in a more positive direction with startling speed.

Ultimately, it all comes down to how we interact with our kids. Simply put, our behavior toward our kids is the cause, and their behavior toward us is the effect. Change the cause and you'll get a different effect!

It is my hope that you'll be able to use the tools and insights you've learned in this book to create a new, more positive relationship with your kid, a relationship that is built on mutual appreciation and respect.

index

about the author

Sean Grover, LCSW, is a psychotherapist with twenty years' experience working with adults and children. He maintains one of the largest group therapy practices in the United States. Sean's other publications include the chapter "What's so Funny? The Group Leader's Use of Humor in Adolescent Groups" in the top-selling clinical volume *101 Interventions in Group Therapy* (Taylor & Francis, 2011), in addition to more than thirty featured articles in two national Buddhist publications, *Living Buddhism* and *World Tribune*.

An inspiring speaker and designer of award-winning youth programs, Sean leads more than 400 groups a year in his practice in addition to monthly workshops in clinics, medical centers, youth organizations, and schools. Sean lives in Manhattan with his wife, daughters, and a bossy Westie named Oliver.

For information on parenting workshops, articles, and videos, or to contact Sean, visit www.seangrover.com.